SO YOU WANT TO LIVE A SUCCESSFUL LIFE?

A journey of discovery for what success means to you and how to get it.

SHRAVEEN RAMDHAR

Copyright © 2024 Shraveen Ramdhar

All rights reserved. This book or any portion thereof may not be reproduced or used in any manner whatsoever without the express written permission of the author.

First Print: 2025

ISBN: 978-1-0370-2274-6

Printed and Bound in South Africa by Print on Demand
Typeset and Cover Design by Carien Human

The author can be contacted at: snramdhar@gmail.com

Acknowledgements

Most undertakings will require support at some stage and in a variety of ways. Meaningful endeavours are those that are shared with the people that matter the most in our lives. I encountered many people that influenced me in different ways. Thank you to all of you for putting me through my paces – positive and negative – because each was an opportunity to better myself. To those that offered negative experiences to me, although the growth was one-sided (in my favour), I collected those "stones" to reach my goals. I hope that this book adds value to you too.

Knowledge truly is power, but applying that knowledge for the betterment of mankind and Mother Earth is, for me, freedom. While trying to acquire as much knowledge as I could, I came across many profound messages. One among the many still resonates with me because it addresses knowledge and education, and read that "The end point of education should be character, not ego" (Sri Satya Sai Baba). A special thank you to all my educators (formal and informal), coaches, mentors, specialists and authors for sharing your knowledge – it made a strong impression on my life.

Relationships are a vital part of our lives so a huge thanks to the people that helped me on my journey to date and with this book. Family is important so here's a shout out to my parents, parents-in-law and siblings.

To my children, you are my conscience and an important source of happiness to us – your parents. Keep growing and making us proud by being the best versions of yourself each day.

To the inspiration behind this book – my wife, who not only supported (and continues to support) my goals, but often pushed me to persevere. The topic of writing this book came up several times – including while I was writing this book. Thank you for always being my centre.

And last but not least, thanks to Carien - my designer - for your patience and professionalism!

Foreword

This book is an account of the path that I followed to reach my goals. Coming from humble beginnings in a single income family to graduating as an engineer, working for some of the best organizations in country, taking on executive roles in prominent companies and ultimately owning my own businesses – all by choice. I call this my success story, which I achieved by starting with my vision for success then following a carefully constructed plan that I believe worked for me.

I hope to inspire you through my accounts but will share that this journey requires dedication, effort, discipline and perseverance. Without giving away what will be discussed in the book, it is important for me that you understand why I say that this worked for me. I stopped conforming to societies views of success and found more value in clarifying what success meant to me. Once I did this and started my journey, life threw many curve-balls, challenges and rewards at me. While it was not always fun navigating the challenges, I will share that I am happy with what I achieved and would not change any part of my life – save for one personal matter that bears no relevance to my success story. Perseverance and embracing all challenges built me to the person that I am proud to be today. My definition of success goes beyond the material or status, but has everything to do with inner peace and mental satisfaction.

As always, there are no guarantees in life. This book is no exception because it will not guarantee that you will reach your potential or that you will get to the top level that you envision for yourself. If you embark on this journey, you will move closer to personal fulfillment and self-improvement. The journey will capacitate you to be better and to want to always better yourself. Even if the prize at the end of the journey does not present itself to you, you will be able to fight for the prize when the opportunity does present itself. Rather be ready to extend yourself because you have the tools than needing the tools when the moment presents itself but you are not ready.

At this point, the obvious question would be whether this book is about self-management. This is definitely not the intent or message of the book. The book will require you to adopt certain principles of self-management to create focus and direction. While I do not cover the principles of self-management, if you have these skills, you will extract more value from this book. If you do not know the traditional self-management techniques, this will not be a problem.

If you are serious about your life and want to become the best version of yourself, I offer you a route that worked for me. My intention is to deliver a "how to" guide for you to set a target, establish a path and embark on a journey to become a high performing functional member in your family, society, organization and for yourself. If you adopt the content shared, I sincerely hope that you use it to be a better version of yourself and look to improve yourself daily – all for the positive.

After streamlining the approach and testing the various parts through my career, I felt comfortable to share the same with as many people as were willing to share in my experiences and knowledge. There were mixed results with some noticeable differentiators between those who experienced positive results and those with less positive results. Based on observations and feedback received, success with the approach is based purely on your honesty with yourself, your desire to be your best, the effort that you are willing to put into yourself and the discipline with which you tackle the challenge to be better.

After many years and many journeys, I opted to share my thoughts through this book with the hope that you will extract as much (hopefully more) value as did I. Accordingly, the approach is applicable to anybody, at any age, in any career and at any stage of life. Whether you are in school looking at your bright future ahead, if you are in an established career, you want to change careers or at the end of your career looking for the next challenge, I believe that the approach and process will be of value to you. As you will see, the value is the process and results from the various elements that will be discussed will differ because your results will be a consequence of your experiences and your actions. Therefore, you will be able to move between the various parts of the process, if required. I recommend following the process fully so that you extract maximum value for yourself.

The time to reach your vision of success will be different for all journeys. Remember to share your knowledge to help improve the lives of the people around you.

Table of Contents

Acknowledgements
Foreword
Part 1: The What?   1
    1   Introduction   1
    2   My Defining Moment and Picture of Success   5
    3   What lies ahead?   11
Part 2: Why?   13
Part 3: The How?   16
    4   The Process   16
    5   Discovering Step 1: Who am I?   23
    5.1   The Important-Interesting Matrix   24
    5.2   Your Circle of Influence (Adapted from Kurt Lewin)   29
    5.3   Self-Reflection   33
    5.4   Feedback from Trusted Sources   38
    5.5   Scientific models   40
    5.6   Self-development literature   42
    5.7   Summary of Step 1   42
    6   Determining Step 2: What do I want?   44
    6.1   Brainstorming   48
    6.2   Rationalizing   54
    7   Actioning Steps 3 to 5: How do I get what I want and where do I start?   62
    7.1   Prioritizing Objectives   62
    7.2   Establishing Goals – The Path to Achieving the Objectives   70
    8   My Life Plan   78
    8.1   Increasing the Life Plan's Utility   84
    9   Bringing it All Together – The 3-Page Plan   89
    10   Measuring and Monitoring Your Performance   90
    10.1   The Value of Measuring and Monitoring   95
    10.2   Measurement and Monitoring Overview   95

| 10.3 | The Detailed Measuring and Monitoring Plan | 97 |

Part 4: Becoming Your Best Self — 111

11	Dealing With the Emotions Around Your Life Plan	112
12	Time to Get Going – the Most Important First Step	117
12.1	Considerations When Taking Your First Step	117
12.2	Taking the First Step	119
13	Moving to the Second Step and Beyond	125

Part 5: Take Stock and Adjust — 130

Part 6: The Extended/Advanced Life Plan — 135

| 14 | Closing Remarks | 138 |

References — 139

Figure 1 - 5-Step Plan to Carve a Path to Success	21
Figure 2 - The Interests-Importance Matrix	24
Figure 3 - Circles of influence, (Adapted from Kurt Lewin)	29
Figure 4 - The compromise for when defining what I wanted	44
Figure 5 - Example of a Personal Development Plan	51
Figure 6 - Example of a Professional Development Plan	53
Figure 7 - Example of removing duplicate ideas	56
Figure 8 - Example of creating themes and scratching related ideas	58
Figure 9 - Example of Rationalized PDP	59
Figure 10 - Example of Rationalised PrDP	60
Figure 11 - Life Plan Hierarchy and Relationship	70
Figure 12 - Quantified goals for prioritized objectives	74
Figure 13 - Example of a Life Plan	81-82
Figure 14 - Example of prioritized and linked life plan	85-86
Figure 15 - The 3-Page Plan to Achieve Your Vision of Success	90
Figure 16 - Iceberg Principle as Foundation for Success	114
Figure 17 - Indicative Schedule to Develop My Life Plan	123
Figure 18 - Indicative Timeline to Develop My Life Plan	124

Table 1 - Example of results for a self-reflection exercise	34
Table 2 - Table of Prioritized Objectives	64
Table 3 - Sorted list of prioritized objectives	66
Table 4 - Possible measuring and monitoring milestones	99
Table 5 - Proposed milestone and progress monitoring	101
Table 6 - Example of tasks (or actions) linked to goals and objectives for measuring progress	103-104
Table 7 -Progress Management	105-106

Part 1: The What?
Introduction

I've always been told to make my passion my job and I'll never work a day. This advice sounded philosophical and when I learned later that this advice was adapted from Confucius, it became an unconscious mantra that I shared in many conversations. While I don't disagree with the statement, I often found myself scratching my head when trying to decipher what it actually meant for me. As a teenager at that time, we were told to get a good education then get a good job and grow within that company. My concern was that life around me was changing and many of the adults that offered advice to me didn't seem to evolve with the times. They preferred to continue doing what they knew best and apply their knowledge to as many situations as possible. While many tried to convince themselves that their ways worked, it was evident that most knew that their ways were fast becoming obsolete and they had to change to stay relevant. I suspected that while most knew that change was necessary for them, most didn't know how to make the necessary changes that would align with the fast-paced changing world around them. This is a very scary place to be – especially as a youngster who was instilled with this mindset and knows little else. Two things were clear for me – I had to do something different, and I had to define what "different" meant for me because life at that time was evolving too fast to continue with that mindset.

Right about now, I imagine that the Millennials (as Sarah Cottrell describes) will be shaking their heads in response to what they would perceive to be a lack of adaptation. Millennials, bear in mind that the Generation Z and Generation Alpha will also be shaking their heads over the views of the pre-1996 generation because "disruption" characterises their lifetime. Disruption, for me, means a different way of thinking, behaving, acting and delivering – not simple changes as would be dictated by adapting. More news, this time for all three generations, you find yourself in a similar situation as the "Greatest Generation" and "Baby Boomers" (again, as Sarah Cottrell describes). Current circumstances demand fundamental changes such that new ways of living and earning a living have to be discovered – exactly the situation that the two early generations faced. My message here is that all generations are in the same proverbial boat and all are trying to deal with disruption that is foreign to everybody. The advantage for this timeline is that there is the benefit of advanced technology and the presence of a precious few that have experienced such changes and are willing to share their perspectives.

Change is inevitable and we can choose to ignore it at our peril or we can choose to embrace the change so that we remain relevant now and for the times ahead. This brings forth another perspective: stop trying to make all mistakes yourself or trying to tackle the world alone – learn from the experiences and mistakes from people that did things before you. Never before has the phrase "knowledge is power" held true than current times, and possibly for the foreseeable future.

Back to my dilemma, the head scratching became more intense and somewhat demotivating to the point that I started to second guess myself and accepted life as it was. Fortunately, the thought of creating a better life remained, which was reinforced by my father as he consistently made reference to his efforts being geared to provide a better life for "the family". The unexpected happened in 1992, when I had my first revelation that helped me to decode these statements and understand my dilemma. After my 1992 revelation and the learnings that followed, I developed a different mindset with three simple streams:

1. Find out who you are.

2. Find out what you enjoy – make this your hobby (or hobbies).

3. Find out what you're good at – make this your job.

The revelation was great but I found myself in familiar territory again – more questions. This time I had some answers, which motivated me to push forward. There were good days and bad days, and the good days seemed fewer and further in between. I tried applying many learnings from my research and received different results which did not help much – or so I used to think. The positive results gave me the inspiration to continue searching – especially since the idea of being successful evoked strong emotions and positive vibes. I was not sure if these achievements would be useful in the long run or if the lessons from perceived failures were worth keeping.

While every person searches for "success", the definition of success is often missed or misunderstood. There's one perspective that equates success to societal standards and another that pairs success to personal standards. In almost all circumstances, the journey to success starts with some defining moment. Some experience this out of desperation, others through proactivity and some through sheer happenstance.

Regardless, the journey to success can and will only start when we experience a defining moment which leads us to create clarity around our definition of success and how this will shape our life. The sceptics would argue that success doesn't always need a defining moment as a catalyst and people are able to choose. I prefer to think that any person that chooses to be successful, will have experienced a defining moment. This defining moment may be small, more personal and not necessarily an earth-shattering moment.

Now for the other bad news, wanting to be successful and being successful are very different concepts. To be successful, action is required. To be successful in a manner that is meaningful to you, requires focused action. Crudely put, only once you know where you are, where you want to be and accept that you need to take action, will you be able to plot a path that will get you to your intended destination. Until that time, one has effectively arrived (metaphorically). If you are happy with where you are then all good – you are successful – please share the rest of my journey through this book. If not, time to take focused action.

My Defining Moment and Picture of Success

My defining moment surfaced as early as 1990 at a family gathering. This was the moment when I started to understand the difference between people's intent and their behaviour. Without going into the details, I decided thereafter that I needed to make a success of my life so I would be able to navigate people's negativity with pride and satisfaction. That defining moment and my actions thereafter led to my revelation in 1992 and laid the foundations for my vision of success.

While it felt good to make that decision, many "why" and "what" questions surfaced. Reality struck again to unearth the vast difference between deciding to be successful and taking the steps to become successful. My overriding thought was the "what" – which occupied a large portion of my thoughts for a long time. At this stage, I knew that I had to squeeze a trigger but had no idea what tool to use because I had no target in sight.

As with all youngsters at that age, we are equipped with the knowledge imparted to us by our small social network of parents, teachers, close family and friends. I decided to reach out to my "network" to get answers to the many questions that I had in mind. The obvious concern was that life was changing for all of us so how useful will those sources of information be? I was comforted with the realization that even though life was changing on a global scale, my network had more life experience than I and presented a source of insight that I would be able to use somehow.

It was overwhelming to see the many different ideas of success and the unprecedented views from others for what I should do with my life and what success should look like for me. Needless to say, most of those views did not resonate with me because it was their views for my life and mostly mis-aligned to what I felt was in my best interest. The best advice came from my parents to "find yourself then do what makes and keeps you happy." For me this meant creating clarity for who I was as a person then discovering what excites me and what will keep me inspired (my definition of happiness). The senior members of my social network consistently emphasised the need to read – all type of books. It was humorous that none of them considered school work as reading but rather the absolute minimum, contrary to my thoughts at that time. Regardless, I understood their message: if I was serious about making a success of myself, knowledge was the critical first step.

I received answers in various forms and over extended periods of time. While this was frustrating, I had the feeling that I was getting closer to decoding this mystery behind creating success for myself. Information became a high priority for me but was daunting because I chose a very wide subject to explore. I turned to the only information source that I knew at the time – school, particularly the school library.

While I felt strong that school was an important stage for development, I believed that school was a necessary stepping stone that didn't prepare scholars sufficiently for life. After swallowing my pride, I spent a little more of my free time (alone) in the school library and indeed some time in the community libraries. Those visits proved that I had a myopic view of school because school offered more value than I had initially considered.

I learned a little about self-help, business, finance, engineering and research – all experiences that influenced my views about school. My take away was the learning process and how inspired I became with learning new ideas, concepts, information and a multitude of other topics.

I was particularly interested in engineering, business, finance and decision making (what I later realised to be strategy) and started to read widely into these topics. I stumbled on self-development and found strange inspiration from some of the content – even though I didn't understand most of what was written. The learning process was a form of self-help but I soon realised that self-development was more than information and general knowledge – it was about using the knowledge to add value to myself, my community and a larger audience. The knowledge was great, but I still had no picture for what I needed to do to become successful. Unconsciously, my journey towards my personal success started and was getting more exciting with every new learning experience.

There were many lessons, some negative but all useful. Most times I did not understand the lesson, only to have life exert its divine force to reveal what I missed through some action, interaction and personal experience. In fact, I discovered the painful fact that one learns more through set-backs (note, not failure) than first time success. For those happy instances of first-time success, I often found myself with more queries than answers or celebrations. At some stages I questioned if I was a sceptic for not enjoying my success. I later realized that this was not scepticism but a desire to want to know more – more about myself, my perceived limits and more about the subject. I felt myself asking a few key questions like: is this all? Is there more? How can I do better? Have I become another statistic by reaching some glass ceiling? As magnificent as our brain is, the brain will always exercise its right to create as many scenarios as it can – or is allowed to create. As exciting as this sounds, for me, it represented a source of chaos that led nowhere – another equally frustrating situation because my vision of success remained blurred.

I started to understand that while I enjoyed learning new topics, certain topics are interesting but not important. Others were interesting and important; not interesting but important while some were not interesting and not important. I defined important topics as those topics that I felt would make me happy if I pursued these and those that I saw myself continuing as I continued with life. The downside to my process thus far was that there was a wealth of knowledge split into varying degrees of interest and importance but no idea how to use that information. My research brought me to a crossroad where I could move forward to create my vision of success; I could turn-around to forget the journey altogether or go left (and/or right) to continue gaining knowledge but have little idea what to do with that knowledge. The fifth option was to stay where I was, which also meant giving up because it was a "do nothing" option. As confusing as this was, I decided to forge forward and embrace what was to come my way.

Reflecting on the process, I expanded my knowledge base and when I applied this knowledge, there was positive and sometimes negative results. It made sense to sift information from my experiences that was important and interesting as a means of finding what success meant to me. Irritatingly, this decision led to other crossroads needing more stop or go decisions – but, it was comforting that the crossroads were popping less frequently.

Stopping was easier only for the immediate term and detrimental to the short, medium and long-terms. The most beneficial option was always to move forward because the sense of satisfaction at the end of the journey made all the trials worthwhile. Each effort and action gave me more clarity for what mattered to me. This made the decision-making process easier because I was starting to answer my "what" questions.

In answering the "what" there grew a greater sense of purpose and perspective. Additionally, any "what" that was positive and/or functional led to a higher sense of fulfilment and added value to more than just myself. It raised other questions, primarily: what does all this learning mean to creating my success story? What was my purpose and what purpose will take me to my success? These questions grew stronger with all the reading and became a loud internal voice that consistently asked: what are you doing and why? That question is enough to break one's spirit and detract from the journey. The difference now was that there were answers and options that resonated with me.

After many years of mulling these questions, I found myself towards the end of my high-school career, around 1995. While I didn't carve out my path to success (or so I thought), I did confirm through my reading and research that I really wanted to be an engineer, with a deeper desire to be a chemical engineer, enter the business world through engineering and make big decisions. Thankfully the first step was clarified early – get into a reputable university to study engineering and then tackle the world one step at a time. I'm not saying that you need a university degree to be successful, what I'm saying is that you need expertise to be successful. Once you have answers to what you want in life, get expertise in the fields that will get you what you want. I opted to get an engineering degree as my first step and I would encourage you to find out what mechanism(s) would work best for you to be knowledgeable in any subject that you choose.

After completing my engineering degree, I entered the real world as an employed person. Reality struck again and reminded me of how much more learning I needed to do before being able to tackle the world. These lessons helped me to refine my picture of success and to create a path to success that showed me what I needed to accomplish along my journey.

In 2004 I had my second revelation. Thereafter I had a strong idea of what success looked like for me, how this would interact with the real world and what I needed to do to realize my vision of success. I defined success as being financially free, generate keen understanding of finance, become a top executive, running my own consultancy business as a recognized specialist, having a close family (wife and kids) and travelling the world. My vision of success was clearer and I determined that the path to my vision of success started with my engineering degree. This was an important stepping stone that would lead to real world experience with multiple industries, develop strong understanding for projects (being short term endeavours), get formal project management training, secure a Master's in Business Administration (MBA) and build the courage to make big decisions. For my vision of success, these achievements would satisfy my need for growth, expertise, running my own business and an investment portfolio of liquid and fixed assets. Easier said than done – even easier to preach.

Without boring you with further details, I'm proud to share that I achieved my vision of success. I obtained a degree in chemical engineering, obtained a project management diploma, obtained an MBA degree, worked in power generation, water, mining & minerals processing, management consulting, rail and port logistics. I was head-hunted multiple times and worked for eight different companies in public and private sectors. During this time, I grew to executive levels, where I interacted with chief executives, heads of companies and ministers to influence strategic decisions at company and country level. It was not easy; there were challenges at every corner and I consistently found myself out of my comfort zone. This roller coaster is scary when the events occur, but always works for the best if your intentions are true.

What lies ahead?

At each stage of my journey, I understood the adage about finding another mountain once you climb your current mountain. The difference for me was that I had some semblance of a formula that worked for me and gave me most of the expected returns. Make no mistake, the plan that I started with in 1992 and then refined in 2004 was not exactly what I achieved at the end. The journey helped me to understand myself better and improve the plan to something more valuable to me than what I started in 2004. Fast-forward to 2024, I've achieved my goals and true to the original plan – I've established a new set of goals to scale the mountain that I found after scaling the first mountain. This was exhilarating (but scary) and established a new higher order purpose for me.

When I reflect, it is clear that the roller coaster of positive and negative results was instrumental to becoming who I am today and made the journey to my destination worthwhile. Each time that I reflect on my life, I come to the same conclusion that I wouldn't change a thing. Sharing my knowledge and giving back are among my goals – so too was being published. My path showed that I could achieve these goals with a single action. More importantly, the path showed the value of mentoring, coaching and support from loved ones because these networks offer a different perspective. I found that each engagement with trusted people helped to clarify my thoughts and simplify my ideas for action. To share my knowledge, give back and be published, the idea to author a book appealed to me.

Recall that this book is a record of what worked for me in my life-long journey to success. There is no guarantee that it will work for you, but if you adopt the principles, you will find out what will work for you. Keep this in mind as I share my message with whomever is willing to listen/read. The obvious question at this stage is: "so what and what now?" The ideas that I share with you through this book will hopefully answer those and more questions, while inspire you to carve a path to your vision of success.

Part 2: Why?

This question – especially when dealing with personal development/self-improvement/leadership – has to be among the most cryptic of questions. As simple as the question is, it is riddled with ambiguity and is sufficient to irritate and detract most people. For me (and for this book), it is not about why I think this approach will work for you, less about why you may or may not be at your peak level and even less about why you should listen to my recommendations. I pose this "why?" question to you for you to answer for yourself, starting with first understanding why you chose to read this book.

Some readers may consider this book to be a quick read, others may be intrigued with "yet another personal development/self-improvement/leadership book", some may be keen to refute my thoughts shared, some may be looking for nothing more than a book to read without taking further action and some may genuinely want to find a way to be a better version of themselves. As I said earlier in the book, this is not a silver bullet and offers no guarantees for success, it is an account of what I believe worked for me and, in my view, can work for you. Through my experiences I hope to offer to you an early opportunity to shape your life and grow to better versions of yourself throughout your life.

This brings me to two "why?" questions for you. The first of which is: Why are you reading this book?

If you are part of the group that want a quick read or a read without further action – my thanks to you and I sincerely hope that you extract some value from the book.

If you prefer to analyse if this is yet another personal development/self-improvement/leadership book, I hope to have changed your mind by sharing an account of what I achieved and why this mattered to me. More importantly, I hope to inspire you to move from this category of reader to the category that applies what I share within this book.

If you prefer to refute my thoughts and ideas, I would congratulate you on the research that you have done to be able to make those assertions and welcome your criticism. For it is only through feedback that we may all grow to become better versions of ourselves. If you choose to keep your views to yourself, I'm good with that too and I thank you for taking time to read my book.

If, however, you fall in the latter category and are sincerely looking to become a better version of yourself, please accept this as a challenge that I believe could work for you. I have no interest in comparing other plans or programs because each program has its strengths and will add value to you if used as those were intended. I will share that I've read many such books and use elements from many books for the value that they added to my journey. This book will not identify the error of your ways, if any, because only you know your experiences thus far and without all facts, there can be no diagnoses or recommendations.

If you fall in any other category, please accept my thanks for getting thus far with the book and I hope to make a compelling case for you to read the book to completion.

For my second "why?" question: why would you not want to

become a better version of yourself?

If you're happy with where and who you are, can you be more?
If you want to be a better version of yourself, this book offers a potential route to achieve this for yourself. I won't be arrogant and call this book "the solution", but it certainly is a means because it worked for me.

I hope to take you on a journey of discovery and will highlight the value of a holistic approach. Effectively, this is a process that starts with you, develops into clarifying what you want, progresses to defining how to get what you want, identifies the actions needed to better yourself, confirms the value accrued to you and then review to improve further. It sounds like a lot of work, but as with life, this is a marathon and why shouldn't you go for gold?!

Part 3: The How?
The Process

This section explains the process that I followed so that you get a sense of what you will be doing as you progress through the book. The chapters that follow will show you how I applied the process to reach my answers. I use models and frameworks that are visual so that you can contextualize your thoughts and ensure that you are being honest with yourself. Hint, you will know if a particular idea resonates with you once you categorise that idea within the model or framework. I urge you to trust the process and review your answers once you complete a particular exercise. Thereafter move to the subsequent chapter or exercise without returning to any particular exercise. You should review your responses once you've completed all exercises otherwise you will be fooling yourself. I made the mistake of going back and forth with certain exercises, which resulted in me taking twelve years (1992 – 2004) to get to the plan that delivered real value to me.

To accelerate your timeline, it is vital that you are clear with yourself about what you want and your motives for embarking on this journey of continuous self-improvement. You will have to dig deep until you get a settling sense of who you are as a person. There is no right or wrong answer and neither is there a noble answer to this question so avoid going down that path. Be brutally honest with yourself because if you opt for a "right" or "noble" answer instead of the truth about yourself, you will create a future that does not work for you. Unfortunately, this is not a class taught at school and nobody tells us how to get this done. To assist, I will share some tools and techniques that I picked up over time and those that I found useful.

Start your journey by determining the things that are important to you, the things that make you happy and also understand your personality profile. You are decoding yourself so you are the expert. Be sure not to take somebody else's perspective for what you want and what will make you happy. Soliciting their input won't hurt, but make sure that you answer this for yourself.

Once you have a better sense of who you are and what you want, the obvious question is how do I get there? This I suppose is the difference between dreams and goals. My opinion is that dreams stay in your head and often forgotten until that memory is triggered at some future time. Goals on the other hand are measurable, clear and can be made specific. The link, for me, is that everything should start with a dream (and dream big), translated to "what you want" then broken into goals. Completing this exercise will create purpose and a big, bold, bright target. Don't be concerned if you don't have a dream or can't remember your dreams about what you want in life because life has a habit of giving multiple routes for the same destination. Use this to your advantage and work with what you have. Being the beginning, the start will be slow – I've experienced this – but speeds up as you progress. I found that reflecting over a few days on each topic and the ideas that I jotted helped stimulate more ideas and thoughts. Who knows, you may even get that dream or determine other topics that you think will help define who you are. Note, reflection is different from going back and forth.

While you might be excited after having a better picture of who you are, let me remind you that this is only the beginning. Your excitement may be short-lived or you may hit a brick wall in the form of a mental block. Don't despair, there is a way around this and it's simpler than most people think. I found that committing your findings to writing is an important step in the process because it creates visual commitment to yourself, while also allowing your inner being to expand on your dreams and goals.

The missing element is the "how" for the dream and goals phase. As always, it's easier said than done and nobody offers a mechanism to get this done. I found that a brainstorming exercise is most useful at this stage, which we will discuss later in this book. The take away here is Stephen Covey's advice to "begin with the end in mind", meaning to start by defining what you want for yourself explained as dreams and goals. My brainstorming session took me approximately six weeks and I went through multiple sessions. Each time that I thought I'd reach the end of ideas, more ideas popped until I reached the stage where I had about two A4 pages of ideas. I took this point as my end because I noticed that I started repeating many ideas. You may generate more or less ideas, but I found that when I applied myself with undivided attention, the ideas flowed easier. My view is that you should extend yourself to more than ten ideas. Even if you use ten ideas as a target, you will likely generate more ideas, which will take you closer to what you think success looks like for you.

Now that the pretty picture for your vision of success is created, visualized and written down, you are ready to move to the next stages. Metaphorically, you reached the stadium where the game of your life is going to be played – but you are still in the parking lot within touching distance of the stadium. To move from the parking lot into the stadium to your seat, you are going to need a route with defined stages and land marks. This is what called my Life Plan – yet again, we will get to the "how to" details later. Expect that the route (aka plan) will have many obstacles between the parking lot, the entrance booth and getting to your seat in the owner's box – not the stands – because in your life, you are the boss, not the observer. As always, coaches are important because coaches will help you stay in the owner's box, so choose wisely.

I hope by this time, the approach to carve out your vision of success (aka your success story) is starting to form. If yes, you're probably mulling over obstacles and what these represent. To demystify this, the obstacles represent key moments in your life that you must navigate to prepare you for your rewards. In self-help and business terms, this is the capacity building part of the process. Nobody starts of trained and ready to tackle the world; we all need some form of readiness which would be a likely combination of experience, formal and informal training, mentoring and coaching. As you begin to identify the steps that you need to take to get to your definition of success, you will need to make several decisions that will impact your life for the better or worse. This will involve decisions around friendships, relationships, jobs, roles, environment (meaning locations), health, education and finance (to name the key aspects). If the picture is getting clearer for you, you will understand your path to success (your life plan) and this plan will be instrumental for all decisions that you make going forward. This is the ideal utility of the life plan so make sure that you spend quality time defining the aspects above and avoid regret or abandoning the process. I used my life plan as a decision-making tool for jobs, activities and relationships. While it sounds scientific, remember that you are in control and can use any tool that you need to make the best decision for your life. This life plan is another tool (albeit a vital tool in my opinion) for you.

If you follow my sports metaphor and have been to stadiums before, you will accept that an important next step is to decide which route you must follow. Translated for this book, where do you start with your plan? I've found that an EQ/IQ approach worked for me. The IQ part was to identify, prioritize and rank each part of my plan and the EQ part was about being true to myself about my priorities.

This is a very delicate moment because you will start to feel bad about making decisions for your life while you have friends, family and other relationships that will be affected by these decisions.
A word of advice: accept that you and only you are going to do what's best for you. While there are people out there who will stand up for you, when the proverbial chips are down, people will mostly choose themselves over you. This is not an indictment on human behaviour, it is a natural response so prepare yourself to make decisions that are in the best interest for your life. The intent is to challenge you towards building a better version of yourself through directed action, not to challenge humanity or human behaviour. That said, accept that there are differences between functional and dysfunctional decision making. The process that I describe is about functional decision making.

Functional decision making refers to positive actions with honour that does not aim to cause harm. When people feel hurt by actions that you take to better yourself (functionally), it is most likely because they did not have your best interests in mind or because they are concerned that they will lose whatever you contribute to their lives through your current habits. Again, I am not going to delve into the psychology of this, but I have experienced this on many occasions. Later in the book I share a possible approach to address this aspect without you feeling like you are being selfish or self-centred.

Dysfunctional decisions are the opposite – your actions aim to cause harm. Let me categorically state that this book is intended for you to better yourself and to get (and stay) on the path of functional behaviour.

If you follow the process summarized above, you will have achieved the following:

1. Discovered your true self.
2. Determined what you want in life.
3. Converted the above into dreams then goals.
4. Established a plan to achieve those goals.
5. Prioritized your plan using a ranking system.

Pictures almost always work better to convey a message. Therefore, the items described above are consolidated into a process, **Figure 1**, so that we are aligned for the path ahead.

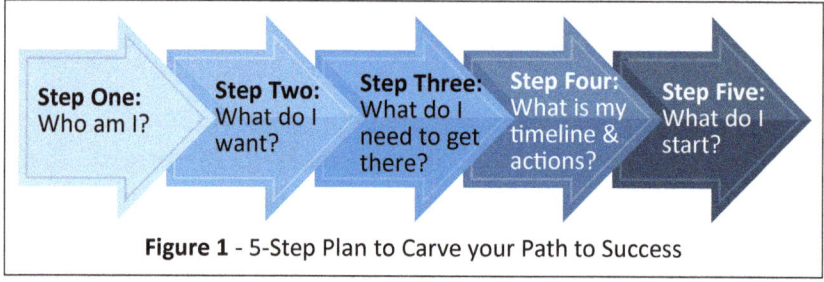

Figure 1 - 5-Step Plan to Carve your Path to Success

As you see from Figure 1, there are five steps and each step aims to get you closer to who you are and what you want in life. Step 5 is designed to use your knowledge and experience to convert your vision of success into reality.

Do not be swayed by the models and illustrations that I use within the book. Their purpose is not to market the models or to look smart, but to demonstrate that value can be extracted from many sources and will always remain value regardless of the application. I learnt the value of appropriately selecting models and frameworks through my MBA degree to create clarity, contextualise solutions then support decision making. These work well for corporates, so when I applied some of the models and frameworks to my plan, I was pleasantly surprised with the value that I obtained.

Now that we contextualised the plan and the value that models and frameworks can add if used appropriately, all that's left is to take action – another very important decision. Waiting too long to take the appropriate action increases the risk to procrastinate or stop the process entirely. To overcome this, start now because "there is no tomorrow!", Apollo Creed (or rather Sylvester Stallone as the writer). This is the first step in your journey and the exciting bit is yet to come so buckle up and push forward.

All effort until now was to create a mental image of the road ahead. Having done that, the next step is to operationalise (excuse my corporate engineering lingo) the plan. This book and the processes described within are not dependent on you needing to read other books to discover your success story then carve your path to success. Should you want to expand your knowledge on certain topics discussed, I whole-heartedly support this and share later some recommended reading. Be prepared to embark on a journey of focussed reading that will contribute more value to your end goal. You will need to prioritize your reading – but take care to ensure that whatever reading you do will give you a sense of fulfilment and accomplishment. When you feel this, you'll know that you're on the right track.

Discovering Step 1: Who am I?

Probably the most difficult easy question that you will be asked. Sadly, very few people are able to answer this question and fewer understand what their answer means to them. I have often been faced with people declining to answer the question for fear of embarrassment or fear of being judged. The longer you put off defining this for yourself, the longer you will wait to achieve your vision of success and the more reliant you will be on blind luck, faith and/or prayer. Faith, luck and prayer are important parts of life, but these are not strategies or plans; and will work for a very small group of people. I prefer the alternative approach to capacitate myself then use luck and prayer to accelerate the opportunities to apply my skills and capacities. There are a few methods that can be used to understand who you are, some of which are elaborated below.

The Interests-Importance Matrix

Over the years in engineering and business we were exposed to many tools. I adapted a tool from the corporate world to contextualize ideas that interest me and those that I deem to be important. The exercise demonstrated where I was spending my time versus where I should be spending my time to achieve my vision of success. **Figure 2** illustrates an example for the interests-importance matrix.

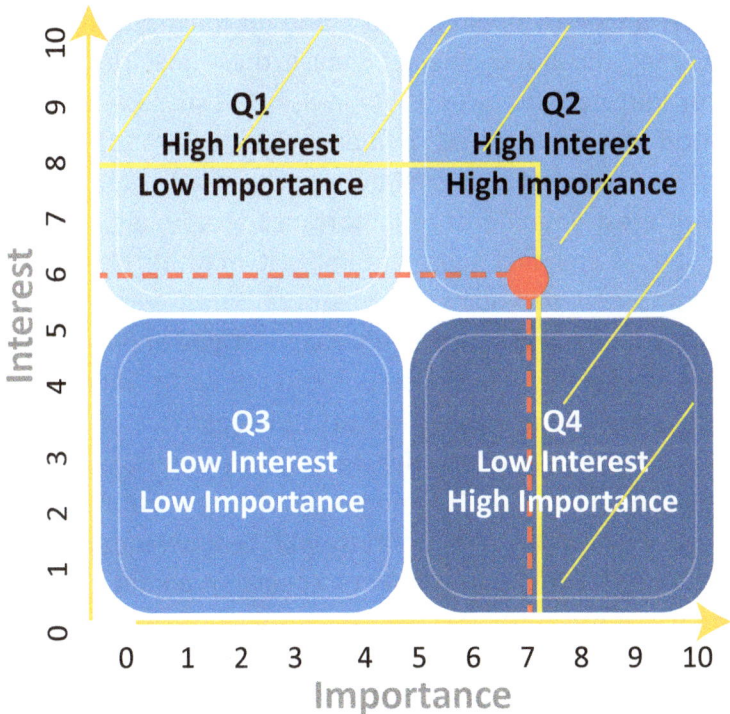

Figure 2 - The Interests-Importance Matrix

Figure 2 illustrates how you may define where you should focus your attention. This model characterises your ideas in intensity of interest and importance to you. The value of this exercise is its simplicity so keep things simple if you choose to do this. Take each idea and give it a score out of ten for interest to you and then a score of ten for importance to you. Plot your scores on the axes to find the intersection point for that idea on the matrix. For example, idea 1 (the red dot on Figure 2) scored six as interest and seven for importance. The red dashed lines show the scores on each axis and how these extrapolate to the point of intersection for idea 1. You will see that idea 1 becomes quadrant Q2 idea and categorised as "high interest, high importance". Once you plot all your ideas, each idea will occupy a quadrant.

All quadrant Q3 ideas should be left alone for now. Quadrant Q1 ideas become your hobby ideas because these inspire interest but may or may not add value to your vision of success. There is all likelihood that Q1 ideas will influence Q2 ideas and therefore should not be discarded but certainly not prioritized. Quadrant Q2 ideas will interest you and have importance to you, e.g. knitting (because it was the first idea in mind), it may be interesting but is it important to your success story? To answer this, ask yourself how knitting will give you success. If you want to be a seamstress or making a business out of knitting or wanting to knit items for people as expression of your feelings, then this is a Q2 idea. If knitting is interesting to you but cannot offer you the creative stimulus to get to your vision of success or a release to rejuvenate yourself, then knitting will be low importance, becoming a quadrant Q1 idea. Q4 is a special quadrant because it shows that these ideas will be vital to your future, but you don't have enough information on these ideas to be certain. These are ideas that you should research further to ensure that you correctly classify their interest and importance. For example, taking a course in finance. Finance will always be important if you intend to be a department head, project manager, own your own business or run a family budget. However, you may not be somebody that enjoyed accounting, statements and reports, and may prefer to stay away from finance. Due to its high importance to you, this means that you should consider doing a course on finance, some supplemental training or research relevant information on finance. Once you develop better understanding of finance, you will be able to finalize the intensity of interest and importance that finance offers to you and how it contributes to your vision of success. This is what makes quadrant Q4 interesting because quadrant Q4, in my opinion, is the second most important quadrant for you. Quadrant Q4 ideas are likely to displace quadrant Q2 ideas and must therefore not be ignored.

The trick is to focus on quadrant Q2 ideas, then quadrant Q4 ideas with importance scores between seven and ten and finally quadrant Q1 ideas with interest scores between seven and ten. The Q1 ideas scoring above seven are important because of their high interest factor, these are likely the ideas that will inspire you to push forward. These limits are reflected in **Figure 2** as the yellow shaded area and is a threshold. This was an important decision because it gave me sufficient time to prioritize and investigate the ideas that mattered to me in about one month. For me, any time longer than one month meant that I was putting my effort in the wrong direction, I was second guessing myself or I was going into too much detail without answering the "question". These are hard decisions that must be made if you are serious about yourself.

As always, models and frameworks look nice but seldom are we clear on how to use these tools with the challenges that we face. When I did the exercise, I came up with many ideas – not all useful – but ideas nonetheless and ideas that needed to be contextualized. Three stood out for me to discuss, namely, "be a family man", "be the boss" and "be a sportsman". When I rated each idea for interest and importance, the ideas scored 8/9*, 6/8 and 7/5 respectively. It took me many days to reach final scores and I had to be strict with myself on most days. Based on my scores, it showed that family life was a priority for me, being the boss was important but I scored the idea low on interest and I loved playing sports but it scored mid-tier for importance because I used sports as a release and for socializing. Based on that, being a family man was a Q2 idea, being the boss was a Q2 idea and being a sportsman was split Q1/Q2 idea.

Based on my categorization, being a family man fell inside my threshold – the yellow shaded area in **Figure 2** – making this an idea that needed pursuing. For this I determined (with support from the important people in my life) that I needed to pursue interests that would strengthen my personal and family life.

Being the boss was important for decision making but low for interest because I placed little value in titles and more value in action. From my engagements and experiences, I realized that I did not need a title to make meaningful decisions. What I needed was recognized and demonstrated competence in a field that was important to me. Being the boss was a Q2 idea and its scoring placed the idea inside my threshold for pursuing as a priority, but its priority was closer to Q3. The scoring showed that there were some aspects of being the boss that were important to me but needed investigation to confirm. This meant that I needed to spend time building skills and competence to make meaningful decisions, not necessarily needing a title.

Being a sportsman was medium-high interest because I loved sports, but wanted to play sports at a social level for the stress release and fitness. The idea was a split Q1/Q2 idea and was placed outside my threshold for decision making. This was an idea that I would keep in mind for health reasons but the priority

*The 8/9 scoring means a score of 8 for interest and 9 for importance.

would be on a personal level rather than a professional level.

Let me not sugar-coat my feelings when I completed this exercise. It was tough, a massive reality check and stressful. I spent many days thereafter reflecting on my decisions and even contemplated adjusting my threshold for decision making. I tested the threshold theory and saw number of ideas to pursue more than double. That scared me even more because it indicated to me that I was not being honest with myself and certainly not being serious about my future. After reinstating my original threshold, I felt a sense of ease because I could see myself being involved with those ideas that fell inside the threshold to select. After more reflection it also dawned on me that I was not discarding ideas, I was prioritizing. Meaning that at any stage as I develop myself, some idea's scoring may change (based on tangible reasons and not just a feeling) and could elevate or relegate around the threshold. This was a comforting realization.

Your Circle of Influence (Adapted from Kurt Lewin)

Probably one of my favourite exercises that must be done alone. This has been a hot debated topic by many leadership specialists and individual development specialists over many years. Although simple, I find its results exceedingly useful because it gives you clarity on the company that you keep, which itself is insight into who you are, see **Figure 3**. I strongly recommend that you complete this exercise for yourself. I've found that including names in the circle is an important part of the exercise and increases the exercise's value to your journey to success.

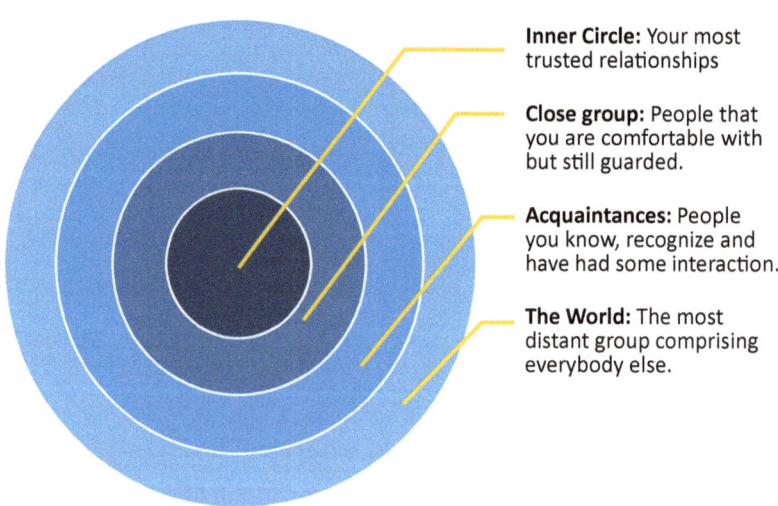

Figure 3 - Circles of influence, (Adapted from Kurt Lewin)

Most notable from **Figure 3** is that the circles get bigger as these move away from the centre, which is where you reside. I cannot stress enough the importance of this aspect because it has been shown time and again that we often fail because we said too much to too many people too soon. Remember, not everybody is out for your success, most don't care, some sit on the proverbial fence and a (very) precious few will be with you unconditionally. My advice will always be to keep this in mind and keep your inner circle small. This works for me in the manner that I describe the circles (below).

The Inner circle is my most intimate circle comprising immediately family, close friends, specific professionals. This is the group with whom I let down my defences because they will not judge me, they are honest (often brutally honest) with me, expect nothing from me (except my trust and respect) and will be there with me through my most valued activities.

The Close Group is the larger group of friends and family with whom I share details of my life, but no intimate details. While I am comfortable to be myself with this group, I am are guarded to some level and will have some defences ready.

The Acquaintances circle comprises people that I encountered at some stage in my life. This is the professional level where I interact with mutual respect and collaboration. I do not actively seek these people at a personal level and will often work with them when needed for specific tasks.

The World circle comprises people outside the three circles above. These are people that I do not know, do not interact with and have no relationship with them. If I encounter them, it will be for a brief moment and there will likely be no dependency on each other.

When I completed this exercise, emotions frequently got the better of me. The predominant thought was that I was being biased to certain people and relationships, which was unfair and possibly unethical. Let me rest your fears – you are not being biased, unfair or unethical. This exercise is not about breaking relationships but about ensuring that you are clear about the relationships that you have and how these support your life and success story. As a principle, if you have not nurtured any relationship in the past month or longer, ask yourself whether this has taken you away from your goals or closer to your goals. So too, if you have nurtured any relationship in the past month, day or week, ask yourself if this has taken you closer to your goals, taken you away or left you where you are. You will then start to understand why you are where you are and why you are moving in a certain direction. When I did this exercise, I saw that I placed lots of emphasis on family that had not contacted or spoke with me in years – even though I tried from my side. Certain friendships offered no value to me other than to use my capabilities and resources only when they needed. There were some friendships where I felt happier, lighter and more inspired when I interacted with them, while with others I felt more excitement by leaving their company. After completing the exercise, it was clear to me that I was wasting time trying to be liked by people that did not care for me instead of spoiling the people that really cared for me. Not only did this exercise give me perspective on my relationships, it also gave me better insight into the person that I was and if this was the person that I wanted to be going forward.

Yet again, more difficult decisions. Let me assure you that once I made these categorizations and acted on their implications, I simplified my life tremendously. I had more time to focus on the people that matter as well as do the things that supported me to get to my vision of success.

Your journey to success will not be appreciated by most people, most will not care, some will admire your journey and for others it will be a source of jealousy. This means that you will find names that elevate towards the inner circle while other names will distance into the outer circles. In my opinion, this is great news and demonstrates that you are on your journey. To address the elephant in the room – yes, your relationships will change as you embark on this journey so be clear what is important to you from the beginning. Is it you (your perception, values, happiness and inner peace) or is it you living on other people's terms without experiencing your value, happiness and inner peace?

Remember, the relationships that last are the ones that you nurture and the relationships that you nurture are the ones that you want to last. Perhaps the greatest utility of Kurt Lewin's Circle of Influence concept (if it is done properly) is that it will clarify to you what you can and should share with the many people that enter your life and how to simplify your life. I found that the fewer people that knew the most about me, the happier I was. These are tough but important decisions to make as the precursor to this journey.

Self-Reflection

The simplest and easiest start to understanding yourself and the tool that will be the best representation of yourself. Another benefit of the tool is that you will be able to incorporate elements from other tools to describe yourself objectively (external input) and subjectively (your personal opinion). Take some time and reflect on your habits, behaviours, actions and interactions with people. Each input that you make must be backed by evidence so that you avoid sugar-coating who you are as a person. Again, honesty with yourself is vital so that you identify and deal with the real issues needing attention.

I did this exercise a few times and found that I extracted the most value when I included analysis of whom I wanted to be as my future self. Understanding myself at a point in time was important, but this was a one-sided picture and offered half the value to this process. The intent of the process is to grow the best version of yourself as the means to realize your vision of success. This is a forward-looking exercise which makes sense only if you create clarity around the person that you want to grow to be from your current self to your future self.

A word of caution, this is a very personal exercise so be honest with yourself – do not justify or rationalize – be clear and honest with yourself. This should be a mental and written exercise so be sure to record your thoughts and why you think so. I often find that the old school method of pen and paper works most effectively – but I encourage you to find what works for you.

When I did this exercise, I found that I was very hard on myself and underplayed my interactions and habits. I also noted that I exaggerated behaviours and actions to make myself feel good about myself. Here is a simple way of addressing this – record any of the above items and add at least two to three examples when you demonstrated that behaviour. For example, if you believe that you have good interactions with people, take two to three interactions with different people from different social environments and record their responses to you. You can revisit the response to this exercise after completing the next exercise. **Table 1** shows some aspects from my self-reflection exercise.

Table 1 - Example of results for a self-reflection exercise

My Self-Reflection Assessment			
	Who am I?	**Explanation**	**Who I want to be**
My Habits	- I talk too fast.	- When I speak with people they often ask me to repeat myself or to slow down.	- Be patient and listen more than I speak.
	- I am not concerned about my physical appearance.	- I don't match my clothing and dress to my satisfaction rather than the event I am attending.	- Sophisticated, smart and calm.
My Behaviours	- I wait for people to finish what they are saying before I start to talk.	- I make a special effort to wait for people to finish talking and clarify that they are finished before I start to share.	- Disiplined, honourable, honest.
	- I prefer to be quiet and not contribute to conversations unless I am asked.	- I am the quietest person in any conversation. - I find many occasions where I say nothing in a group while others are having a dicussion.	- Outspoken, well-spoken, good communicater. - Principled and assertive.

	Who am I?	Explanation	Who I want to be
My Actions	- I often offer assistance to people without having to be asked.	- I am the first to help other busy with tasks and the first to offer my assistance.	- Focused, easy going and approachable.
	- I am respectful and greet elders, peers and juniors alike.	- I make special effort to greet everybody when I see them.	- Time-conscience, punctual.
My Interactions with people	- I enjoy meeting people in social business and events.	- I enjoy attending functions and feel happy and relaxed in people's company.	- Humourous, comfortable, easy. - Considered, calm, clear.
	- People enjoy my company and look forward to my presence.	- I actively look to join many discussion groups - especially when there are many people.	- Professional.
My Competencies	- Engineering and design (mining, minerals processing, water treatment, power generation and rail systems).	- I have done design work, solution development, construction and management in each sector.	- Technical and business solutions development
	- Business Strategy.	- Involved with business strategy, business case development, EXCO member.	- Techincal and business solutions development.
	- Leadership	- Recognised as a leader with the support of teams outside my organization and department.	- Business Strategy
	- Project Management and functional management	- Appointed department head, project director, program manager and project manager for small, medium, large and mega portfolios,	- Execution and delivery. - Executive management and management

	Who am I?	Explanation	Who I want to be
My Competencies (continued)		- Programs and projects.	
	- Executive Management. - Commercial and contracts management.	- EXCO member, steering commitee member, company representative. - Establish procurement and construction contracts (FIDIC, NEC)	- Finance
My Skills	- Engineereing and Design	- I have done design work, solution development, construction and management in each sector.	- Engineering and Design.
	- Project management and delivery.	- Involved with business strategy, business case development, EXCO Member.	- Project mangement.
	- Management consulting	- Worked as management consultant with a major consulting company.	- Management consulting.
	- Operations management.	- Done power station operations as engineer, operational readiness, operations set-up.	- Operations management.
	- Business case development	- Developed and wrote business cases for programs and projects.	-Business development. - Business management.

As you see in **Table 1**, you can have multiple explanations to each description and multiple descriptions to each category. The trick is not to be constrained about format or correctness, but to capture the reality for yourself with honesty. A word of caution, when you are analysing who you are, avoid recording what you would like to be as a person. Rather take the time to reflect on the reality by purposefully observing yourself over one to two weeks, reflecting daily then recording at the end of each day. Remember, there can be no improvement to perfection, so be weary of portraying yourself to be perfect. Once you have done this you will get a sense if the picture of yourself resonates with you. This will lead you to create clarity around the person that you want to be – hopefully functional and positive – which will be important input to plan your future endeavours.

Feedback from Trusted Sources

This is usually a nerve-wracking exercise, but remains an effective source of information about yourself. The key is to identify a varied group of people from your personal and professional life. Speak with family, employees, seniors at the office, peers, colleagues, friends and people with whom you socialise. There is the risk that you speak with people that are naturally cynical, negative and/or overly positive. The cynics and negative people will focus on your negative traits and may even exaggerate their views – possibly because these kinds of people often feel better when others feel bad.

I engaged people that spoke positively about me and realised shortly thereafter that there is no improvement to perfection but I was far from perfect. I was clearly fooling myself and decided to engage people who were demonstrably objective and a final group that did not enjoy my company. You would think that the words would pour out, but this was not always the case. The group that was not enchanted by me were the most reserved because they were suspicious of my motives. Some offered reluctant feedback and most did not want to be bothered. My view was that all responses were feedback, either from their comments or from trying to identify some of my behaviours that led to them feeling the way that they did about me.

Dealing with the feedback that you will receive is vital. Do not let the feedback bother you to the point that you become obsessed with the feedback and get distracted from your journey. This is a journey of self-improvement to carve out your vision of success, which means that feedback is crucial to the process. If you do not know where you may be sabotaging yourself, where you may need development and/or do not know your strengths; you will not be able to grow into your best self. Anyways, a journey to become your best self will take you to a level of growth where you be able to deal with negative feedback as you progress.

As gut-wrenching as it is to hear people speak negatively about you, recognize that you will have gained insight that you previously did not have into areas needing attention. You would also get clarity on your perceived value to many groups, insight into the company that you keep and most importantly, understanding if this company is working in your favour or against you. Using multiple and varied sources for feedback will give you a sense about the validity of the feedback because you will see patterns emerge. On the positive, as you revisit the circle of influence, you will be able to simplify your inner and trusted circles.

To the contrarian view, as much as we enjoy hearing the positive about us, this may work against you. I find that people who only share the positive aspects are afraid of hurting other's feelings but underestimate the long-term damage that their diplomatic or overly complementary input causes. As shared earlier, there is no improvement needed to perfection, therefore the overly positive feedback can be more harmful than the cynic or negative feedback. Should this happen, there is the real risk that you will stagnate. Although it may be misplaced, negative feedback will play on your conscience and force you into some improvement drive.

I found that identifying people that display objective behaviour and often speak the truth regardless of their company are best to approach. Approaching each person individually added more value for me because there was minimal group-think influence.

Scientific models

There are many scientific models that are available to understand yourself better, namely IQ tests, EQ tests, psychometric tests and the like. I implore you to use a professional who knows what they are doing and are able to interpret your answers properly. This is your life so take it seriously and get people who are serious about the value this will add. Be sure to have proper debriefing with the testing specialists around their findings.

For me, the debriefing worked best in two stages. During the first feedback stage the professional shared their report and findings. This is generally an overwhelming session because you will be hearing things about yourself that you didn't know (understand or accept) and the sheer volume of information will be an overload itself. I found that taking the report away, reviewing it at your leisure then revisiting the professional two to three weeks later – the second feedback stage – after you've processed the feedback added the most value. Try this, you may be pleasantly surprised by what you learn about yourself.

My preference was to avoid the unsolicited online social media tests because there was no backing for the assumptions. I was also sceptical about the purpose behind the test, because I am not a psychology specialist and do not test the inner meaning of the questions. In most cases I found that the tests were used to collect marketing material around consumers' behaviours rather that providing insight into myself. If you choose to use an online platform, ensure that the platform is credible because you will be making decisions on the back of the results.

Self-development literature

I can attest to its value – only if you use a wide source of literature in the form of books, peer reviewed articles and journals. I use many sources for self-development and general reading. For the process that I describe within this book, I found great utility from Stephen Covey's "Seven habits of highly effective people", Spencer Johnson's "Who moved my cheese", Thomas Erikson's "Surrounded by idiots", Chapman's "Five love languages", Robin Sharma's "The monk who sold his Ferrari", Anthony Robbin's "Awaken the giant within", Ken Blanchard's "Winning" and James Clear's "Atomic Habits". While I'm not advocating these authors as a must read to extract the value from this book, the principles that were shared are geared toward understanding yourself better and how to position yourself to be the best version of yourself. This, for me, is the most functional first step of the journey.

Use the information and exercises to create an objective picture of yourself. Be true to yourself with your feedback otherwise you will improve a less functional aspect or ignore a dysfunctional behaviour.

Summary of Step 1

This step of the process will be difficult but rewarding. If you do any of the activities mentioned, you will have gained better insight into who you are. If you do all exercises, the picture that you create for yourself may well be high-definition (HD) quality. Do not overdo this exercise because the information starts becoming repetitive and costly. The moment you start to find repetition and find yourself saying "yeah, I know this" it is time to stop doing additional exercises.

Now that you've understood yourself better, you are ready for the next stage of the journey.

Determining Step 2: What do I want?

Yet another easy question, but is the answer clear and are you happy with your answer? Through my years I spent more time defining the achievable versus what I want, which meant that I settled for a compromise as described in **Figure 4.**

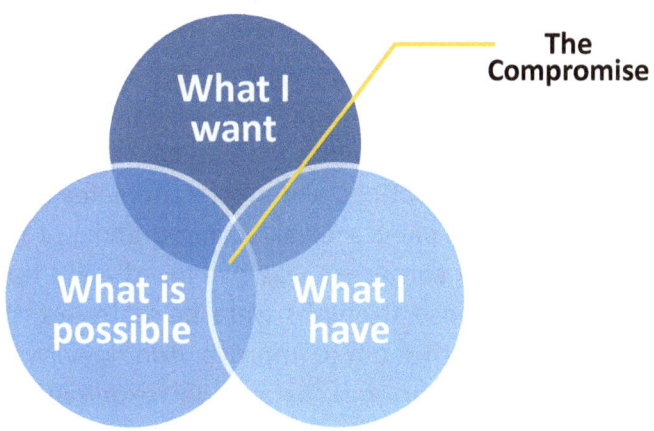

Figure 4 - The compromise for when defining what I wanted

If you have ever felt this way you will understand the unanswered and unclear question that constantly lurks in the back of your mind: "Is this really what I want?". This was exactly where I found myself in 2004 when I had my second revelation that led to my (then) final life plan. Leading to 2004, I had an underlying concern to "find my cheese", as described much later in Spencer Johnson's book "Who Moved My Cheese?". While it was great to be where I was – educated and employed – I was concerned about the unknown-unknown relating to what could go wrong. As a South African, at that time the country was going through massive political changes that created unparalleled uncertainty. My "cheese" could be moved or the environment could change at any time and my "cheese" could be directly affected. This meant that what I have (Figure 4) could change at any time and what I wanted could also be different. The realization set in that even my "compromise" was on thin ice.

I started to question most things in my life and had to be frank with myself about my current state, the changing world around me and what this meant for me. I was looking for options to alleviate my anxiety during a time when a large percentage of the population were going through similar experiences. It was painfully obvious that my support base and options were hit hard and there were more people in my situation than I had ever imagined. Naturally, this meant fewer options and more candidates fighting for those options. While I paint a bleak scenario above, I had two major strengths in my corner – I was employed and I had some skills. Even though those strengths were being tested, they remained strengths but with room to improve. Additionally, I had access to experienced mentors and coaches who experienced life changing events and emerged better from those events.

After taking advice from my experienced networks, I recognised a pattern from those difficult events where people emerged better. Clarity, attitude, competence and agility were among the top characteristics that helped most people navigate their difficulties. Worth noting was that the difficult experiences affected each person's personal and professional lives to varying degrees. When I compared those experiences to what I felt at the time, it was obvious that I had work to do for myself to strengthen my position. The only way that I was going to differentiate myself from the masses with the limited time, was for me to be clear about what I wanted upfront because this would lay the foundation for what I needed to do next and address how I adjust to the changes going on around me. My personal and professional lives had to be improved in parallel.

The good news is that there is a way to overcome this nagging feeling and answer the question for what you really want for yourself and how to get it. This will also give you the capacity to handle difficult career and/or personal situations without losing confidence. Through my research, I realized that I had "a" perspective and not exactly a means to get to my answer. While some questions were answered, there remained unanswered questions and new questions. To address these unknowns, I decided to categorise all that I wanted either as part of my personal life or as part of my professional life. Given the level of anxiety, I decided to abandon limiting thoughts and describe what I wanted independent of other people's views, without consideration of how ridiculous any desire appeared and then generate a short-list to action. This meant brainstorming each aspect to get the creative juices to flow as strong and wide as possible, then rationalize my responses to reach a set of desires (regardless of their scale or likelihood) that would make me happy and inspire myself to aspire for better each day going forward.

Skipping ahead, through my career some of my concerns materialised where my "cheese" was moved and led to anxious times. I survived two retrenchment cycles from two different companies and will share that it was not pleasant. I was exposed to another process where I was under question because I didn't follow "questionable" instructions and was considered to be added to that company's risk pool (the first and only time in my life). There were some personal challenges as well, which I will not share for obvious reasons. Even though things worked out, being considered potentially redundant with some aspects of my personal life being challenged hit at my core. Having clarified what I wanted for my personal and professional life gave me focus and purpose, which took me through those tough periods. Because what I wanted was developed such that I would be happy and inspired upon achieving these, I did not consider abandoning those desires because each time I achieved some aspect of what I wanted, I experienced the benefits. After all, I emerged through my difficulties being stronger and better than I was when I entered those events, so there was no need to consider alternative approaches.

To return to the subject, let's get cracking and define what you really want for yourself.

Brainstorming

As the title suggests, this is a brainstorming exercise, so time to get your mind into gear, grab a pen (or pencil) and paper. The woke generation may disagree with the brainstorming method, but this book is not about that, it's about extracting personal value and directing this to achieve your vision of success. The choice of medium, be it pen (or pencil) and paper; or digitally is immaterial at this stage – the exercise is far more important – so choose what works for you. I tried the traditional and technology approach and prefer the traditional pen-paper exercise because I find that I think better this way.

You may choose to start with your professional or your personal plan. When I did the exercise, I started with my professional life plan and found myself pre-occupied with my personal life. That led to me mixing ideas and some fuzziness around what I was trying to achieve. After some consideration, I stopped with my professional life plan, moved onto my personal life plan and was able to focus much easier. When I returned to my professional life plan, I was able to dedicate proper attention to it because I had already dealt with my personal matters. I did find that I had a few ideas in my personal plan that belonged to my professional plan (and vice versa). Don't worry about this, keep the idea because there is a mechanism to handle this effectively. As a guide, I decided that if every fourth idea belonged to the other plan, then I was pre-occupied with the other plan and had to change. If you find that you are crossing between plans too frequently, make a call for which plan you choose to continue with and stick with that call. If this happens, I suggest that you get to the other plan shortly after completing the plan that you selected because your creative juices are flowing fast and it will add more value to you to keep that momentum. At this point, take a few moments to consider which matters more to you and likely to overshadow the other side. Once you know this, you're ready to start your brainstorming exercise. Given the swap that I made from my professional to personal plan, I opted to continue with the personal life plan for myself and for this book.

Take your selected medium and start writing down everything that you want for your personal life – not what's possible, not what's achievable, not what society says you should have and certainly not what you have at present. If, however you feel that you are clear about what you want, then the exercise should be quick and easy. Either way, I propose that you carry out the exercise anyway to test how life has transformed for you since you last carried out this or any similar exercise. Write each new idea on a new line, don't worry about spelling, grammar, repeating an idea or rationalizing an idea. The intent is to describe what you really want in your personal life that will make you glow and beam a smile that stretches beyond ear-to-ear. Caution, keep your ideas functional and positive – this process is about being a better version of yourself and not only about doing what you want better. The difference is that if you choose only one part – to do things better – you could become a mastermind career criminal, which is definitely not the intent of this book. If however you choose the holistic approach to be a better version of yourself, this relates to doing things better and developing strong functional behaviours.

It is best to do this exercise in solitude, without interruptions or disturbances so that nothing interferes with your creativity. Be wary that if you have a family or people around you, they will most likely want to know what you are doing so be clear that you need some time to yourself. When I had my second revelation in 2004, we had a house full with parents, my wife and a new born son. I opted to carry the exercise out after 10pm but told the family that I was busy with a development exercise and needed solitude. This approach worked for me and may work for you.

When you find that you are running out of ideas, step away from writing and do some other activity – preferably something physical so you engage more of your creativity. I recommend staying away from television, not scrolling on your phone and/or avoiding gaming for the break because these devices are wired to engage you for longer so you're likely to numb your mind periodically. I'm not suggesting that these devices are bad for you – I have my opinions and I'm sure that you have your own opinions to make-up your own mind. For those few times that I engaged these devices during a break, I lost about five hours and had no desire to return to the exercise. It took me several days thereafter to return to the exercise and I had to convince myself of the value of doing the exercise. This is where the pen-paper approach helped me because it was visual, couldn't be stored in some out of sight digital file and was in my line of sight constantly. Being a constant visual reminder got me to get back to the exercise and complete what needed to be done.

There is no time limit for your break so don't try to schedule creativity. Get back to the brainstorming exercise when you feel that you are mentally ready. When you return to the exercise, don't review what you've already written down, pick-up from where you left off – just start writing again. Follow the same pattern to break and return as described above when needed. You will know when you get to the final session because you will find that you would add maybe 1-2 ideas for your personal life. The brainstorming exercise could take one week or as long as two months – depending on your commitment. My process consumed six weeks with plenty of breaks. I found that waiting longer than 2-3 days between sessions is counterproductive and will lose value for you – please keep this in mind.

After completing your personal life plan's brainstorming exercise, your personal life plan should look something like **Figure 5.**

My Personal Development Plan (PDP)

- ✓ Married by age 25
- ✓ 3 kids by age 32
- ✓ Financially free by 45
- ✓ Travel my country before in 2 years
- ✓ Take holidays every 3 months
- ✓ International holiday every year
- ✓ Buy my dream car in 2 years
- ✓ No debts by age 43
- ✓ Visit a different family member every weekend
- ✓ Start my vegetable garden at home
- ✓ Pay my bond in the next 7 years
- ✓ Lose weight in 8 months
- ✓ Start training at the gym in 2 weeks
- ✓ Get a masters degree before age 40
- ✓ Happy wife and kids
- ✓ Get a PhD before age 50
- ✓ Open my own business by age 43
  etc...

Figure 5 - Example of a Personal Development Plan

Note a few things from **Figure 5**, namely:

- There is no structure behind the ideas.
- There is no attention to punctuation, expression or grammar.
- There are repetitions.
- All ideas deal with you outside of your job – even though you may want to start a business, which could be considered professional. Be sure to add that point regardless, this is about brainstorming and creativity, we will get to rationalizing later.
- There are items that could be considered part of a professional development list.
- There is clear focus on what YOU want. Nothing to do with what your parents, spouse, kids, friends and family want.

Again, this is not an exercise to establish selfish behaviour or self-centred mindset, but an exercise to decode what you want in conjunction with who you are. If you achieve this, there will be alignment with your family, friends, partner, spouse and children. The intent is to make you the best version of yourself without apprehension – that can only bring positive and strong relationships.

Now that you're done with the Personal Development Plan (PDP) brainstorming exercise, set this aside and move onto your Professional Development Plan (PrDP). Repeat the exercise and make sure that you use new pages, that is, don't mix with your personal development plan. Once completed, your professional development plan could look like **Figure 6**.

> # My Professional Development Plan (PrDP)
>
> ✓ Qualify as a chemical engineer before age 22
> ✓ Develop certificated professional expertise before age 30
> ✓ Be a project manager by 35
> ✓ Project director by age 40
> ✓ Work in mining, water, power and transportation
> ✓ Be a CEO
> ✓ Join multiple boards as a board member
> ✓ Have multiple income sources
> ✓ Get promoted every 2 years until I become general manager
> ✓ Own rental property in 3 countries
> ✓ Become a recognised specialist in business
> ✓ Understand Finance
> ✓ Understand commercial and contract law
> ✓ Be assertive
> ✓ Be an effective decision maker
> etc...

Figure 6 - Example of a Professional Development Plan

As you see in Figure 6, the same rules above apply. Reminder, do not rationalise, classify or limit yourself; list everything that YOU WANT. The timeline should be similar but having gone through the PDP cycle, do not be alarmed if you go faster through this exercise.

If you try to rationalize your PDP before moving onto your PrDP, you will most likely rationalize your PrDP instead of brainstorm because your brain is wired to simplify and take the shortest/

fastest route to complete any activity. If you do this, you will lose value and will have a plan that describes too little about yourself.

Rationalizing

Now that you have your PDP and PrDP as separate brainstorming exercises, it's time to rationalize (or simplify). The rationalizing step is about creating focus to drive purpose such that every action is directed to deliver value to you in some or other way. When I did this, I found that consolidating and rationalizing led to a smaller group of ideas with independent themes that described what I believed would add value to me personally. My research also showed that we achieve more by doing less at a time because this creates stronger focus on what needs to be done. Rationalizing created clarity of purpose for me and motivated me to take the necessary next steps.

To rationalize your plans, start by removing duplicate ideas, re-allocate ideas between the plans and clarify your ideas with a little more detail. You must be clear on what you mean for each idea. If a new idea surfaces while you are working through your lists, add the idea to the respective list. During rationalizing, you should look to create common themes from all ideas that describe what success looks like for you for each plan. You will also find that some ideas may be a standalone theme, e.g. "healthy lifestyle", while multiple other ideas may need to be combined into a single theme. For example, if you have three separate ideas as "having a wife", "having kids" and "having parents live with you", these may be consolidated into a theme called "Happy family life". At the end of the rationalizing exercise, you should generate a PDP and PrDP that have as few themes as possible, but represents every idea from your respective brainstormed lists. To ensure that you extract as much value from the exercise, the next few lines will take you through the rationalizing exercise. Every reader will have a different level of exposure and experience so this book is written for any person aiming to better themselves. Some aspects may be too detailed for some readers that have done similar exercises in the past. If you fall in this category, I would suggest skimming over the next few lines to extract the process instead of focusing on the details. For those that need the detail, push forward.

Start with any list, let's use the PDP for the purposes of this exercise. Work through the brainstorming list to remove duplicate ideas by keeping the first of the common ideas and scratching out the duplicates. I recommend adding the letter "D" for duplicate next to the scratched duplicate idea in a different colour ink and add which idea(s) that it duplicates next to the "D", as illustrated in **Figure 7.**

> **My Personal Development Plan (PDP)**
> - ✓ Married by age 25
> - ✓ 3 kids by age 32
> - ✓ Financially free by 45
> - ✓ Travel my country before in 2 years
> - ✓ Take holidays every 3 months
> - ✓ International holiday every year
> - ✓ Buy my dream car in 2 years
> - ✓ ~~No debts by age 43~~ D (Financially Free)
> - ✓ Visit a different family member every weekend
> - ✓ Start my vegetable garden at home
> - ✓ Pay my bond in the next 7 years
> - ✓ Lose weight in 8 months
> - ✓ Start training at the gym in 2 weeks
> - ✓ Get a masters degree before age 40
> - ✓ ~~Happy wife and kids~~ D (Married by 25, 3 kids by 32)
> - ✓ Get a PhD before age 50
> - ✓ Open my own business by age 43
>   etc…

Figure 7 - Example of removing duplicate ideas

As illustrated on **Figure 7**, once the duplicates are removed, work through the list again to establish common themes. I found that starting with the first unscratched idea on the list after removing the duplicates then comparing the remaining ideas to this idea worked best for me. When starting with the first (unscratched) idea, choose a theme for that idea and record the theme next to the first idea, then scratch out the first idea. Now compare that theme to the remaining unscratched ideas. As you find an idea that falls best in that theme, scratch that idea out and draw an arrow that links that idea to the theme. This will be the first pass for rationalizing your PDP. With the second pass, take the next unscratched idea from the top of the list, choose a theme for this idea (which we will call the second theme), write that theme next to the first unscratched idea for the second pass, then scratch out the first unscratched idea in the second pass. Now compare the second theme to all other unscratched ideas to find matches – similar to the first pass. Remember to note the common ideas found and draw arrows from the common ideas found during the second pass to the second theme. Repeat the exercise for subsequent passes until you have scratched all ideas and linked each (non-duplicated) idea to a particular theme. This is illustrated in **Figure 8**.

Figure 8 - Example of creating themes and scratching related ideas

In **Figure 8** the content in blue represents the first pass where the first theme was recorded as "Happy family life". The second pass is captured in green, where the theme is recorded as "Financially free by 45". You'll note that a theme may be the same as the idea – this can and will happen. Once completed, you will have a list of multiple themes and all ideas from the brainstorming exercise scratched out as shown in **Figure 9**.

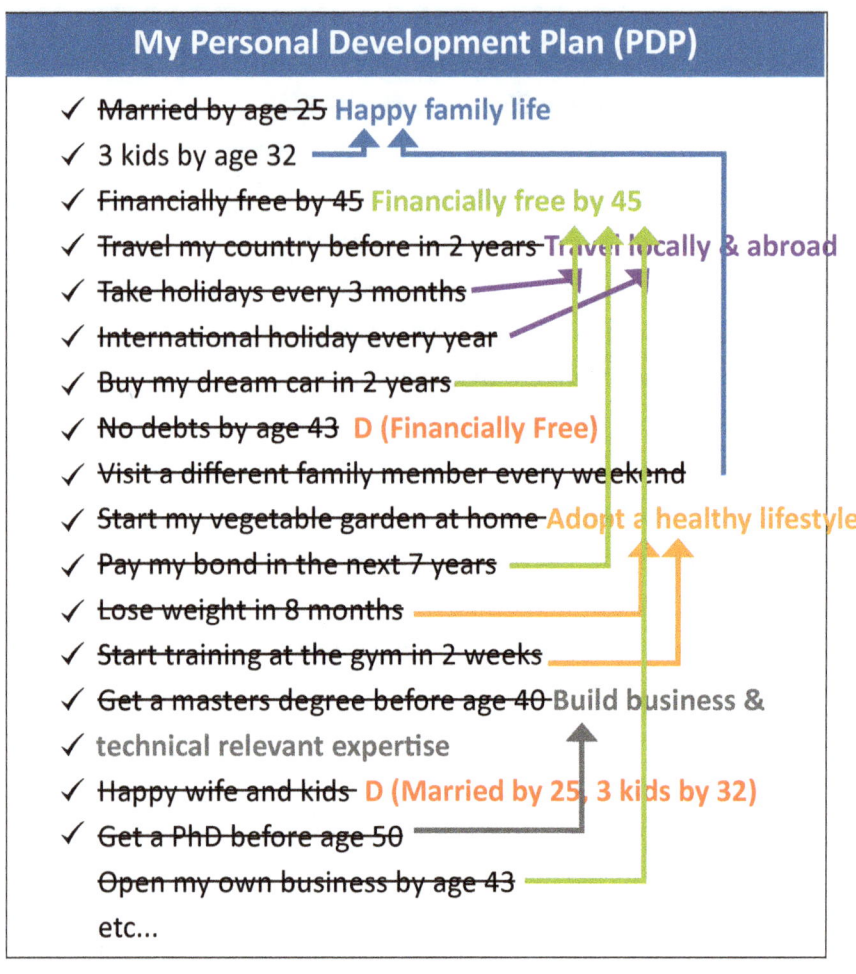

Figure 9 - Example of Rationalized PDP

Figure 9 shows the rationalized list and that the list was streamlined to five themes. These themes now become objectives that you believe will deliver personal success once fulfilled. The objectives will be expanded into various goals that, once achieved for each objective, will mean that that specific objective will have been satisfied. By extension, as you achieve each objective you will take yourself closer to your definition of personal success.

Once you have rationalised the PDP, use the same process to develop your rationalized PrDP, as shown in **Figure 10**.

Figure 10 - Example of Rationalised PrDP

Figure 10 shows the rationalised list to three themes, which will become your professional objectives, then expanded into multiple goals. You will note that there are aspects that will cut across the PDP and PrDP, e.g. income generation and financial freedom. This is good because objectives (or themes) that may be linked will show that the PDP and PrDP will add value to you holistically. If there are no linkages, this is not a problem and means that you will need more time and action to achieve your best self. It is not a sprint; this is a marathon and will take time so that the results are sustainable.

Exercise caution at this stage to avoid large lists of objectives. A manageable number of objectives will add more value and offer better chances for you to take the necessary action. I found that a set of seven to nine objectives in total per plan adds the most value. If you have too few objectives, you run the risk of doing too many things in parallel without seeing benefits in the short-term. Too many objectives indicate that you mixed goals and objectives. Both scenarios are undesired and indicate that you haven't applied your mind sufficiently, which will lead you to abandon the plan in the near future or to inadequate results.

Note
Once all objectives have been achieved you will have achieved success in your personal and professional life. It is natural that you may feel that there may be some missing element. If this is the case, this means that there are other objectives that you may have ignored during the brainstorming and/or rationalizing exercises. Alternatively, this would also signal growth and development, which means that you will naturally have different personal goals and objectives. At this time, it will be important to repeat the PDP and the PrDP exercises and define your new personal goals for your future best self. This is a teaser for what is to come and is covered later, so do not be concerned about it.

Actioning Steps 3 to 5: How do I get what I want and where do I start?

The brainstorming and rationalizing exercises created clarity for what I wanted described as my personal and professional objectives. The exercises did not clarify how I would be able to get what I wanted or how to get what I wanted the most first. This is where I found value in prioritizing – which is nothing more than making sure that I achieved my most important desires first and the rest of my desires in descending order of preference.

As important as prioritizing my objectives was, my objectives are high-level and needed further expanding to define what I needed to do to achieve each objective. This led to establishing goals associated with each objective that will determine what I would do first and thereafter.

Prioritizing Objectives

Arguably the most nerve wrecking part of the journey thus far. This is stage of the process where you have to make hard decisions for where and what to start. I found that it is best to be objective and honest with myself when making these decisions – simply because it was my plan and I did not need approval from anybody to be a better version of myself. I accepted that the actions from the PDP and PrDP will directly affect me and indirectly affect certain relationships. Staying where I was prior to having the PDP and PrDP would not get me to be the person that I want to become. That stagnation, in my opinion, would have a more profound (mostly negative) effect on all my relationships. I used this as motivation to make the hard decision to prioritize.

Until now, everything was about being the best version of yourself in a functional way, so there is no harm is being clear where your priorities lay. Don't apologise for your decisions and selection, but make sure that you are clear for yourself on why you select the priorities for your defined objectives. You will know when you are apologising for a decision because the first thought in your mind would be about what others would think about your priorities. To contextualize that, look around you and reflect who really was with you when you needed the help and support the most. That will give you some indication of the people whose opinions you should consider – and possibly where you need to focus attention for your relationships. Once you clear this mindset you will be ready to establish your priorities, as described below.

Start prioritizing by re-scribing the shortlisted objectives from the PDP and PrDP exercise. I find that using a table format offers the best value for evaluation. Be sure to record which category (PDP or PrDP) that the objective belongs. Once done, assign each objective a score out of 100 – do not use decimals and no objective must have the same score as any other objective, see **Table 2**. I found this to be a difficult exercise and took three days to complete the exercise. During this time, I had to consistently remind myself about why I was doing this – as shared in the paragraphs above.

Table 2 - Table of Prioritized Objectives

Objective Level	Objective	Area	Relative Score %
Ob-1	Happy family life	PDP	22%
Ob-2	Financially free by 45	PDP	18%
Ob-3	Travel locally and abroad	PDP	14%
Ob-4	Adopt a healthy lifestyle	PDP	17%
Ob-5	Build business and technical relevant expertise	PDP	19%
Ob-6	Develop specialist technical and business qualifications	PrDP	0%
Ob-7	Career development to company head	PrDP	10%
Ob-8	Mulitple income sources and financial freedom	PrDP	0%
	Total of weighted scores		100%

Table 2 shows the immediate value of tabulating. You will note that Objective Ob-6 scored 0. This is correct because objective Ob-6 is the same objective as Ob-5 but applies differently to each plan. In this case there is no need to duplicate effort by giving both objectives a score because this will only create a skew-abnormal focus on your growth and journey to success. You can choose which objective category to allocate as the duplicate item then give that objective a score of 0, but DO NOT delete the duplicate objective. Working on the prioritised objective will give the same progress to the duplicate objective. Note also that there are no identical priorities, but there are some that are close to each other in description and intent.

64

This is the stage of the process when I got overwhelmed because of information overload. Admittedly, I questioned whether I was wasting time or adding real value. Let me assure you that you are adding value but having not done a similar exercise before, you will have a fuzzy picture of the road ahead. I took a few weeks to get to understanding the road ahead because of this doubt, but having reached this point and beyond, I was all the happier for completing the exercises.

Returning to the plan, this amount of information about your plan for a successful life and prioritized objectives will raise questions over where to start and if the priorities are "correct". Taking emotion out of the decision gives you the best chance for moving forward and offers you a final opportunity to confirm your priority allocation or adjust the priorities. Remember, it is about what you want for your life so you must be excited about your decisions. If not, you will not take the necessary action on any of the decisions made thus far and you will be less motivated and disciplined – neither scenario will get you to your defined level of success.

Once you have finalised your priorities, it would be better to arrange your priorities in descending order of priority, as shown in **Table 2**. The top two scoring objectives are the primary objectives, the next three are secondary objectives and the remaining set will be tertiary objectives. You will deliver all objectives but will start with the objectives that mean the most to you and will deliver the most value to you. It is not possible to start everything together; even if you are not working, not in any educational institution or don't have a family of your own. If you have all three aspects and choose to do too much simultaneously, this will complicate a simple but effective process which will result in you abandoning the process. To overcome this, I decided to focus my attention on achieving value rather than being busy. I felt this to be a more productive means to achieve my goals and objectives. As

I experienced the value from achieving each goal then objective, this motivated me to continue and push forward. With this in mind, I decided to start with my primary objectives, then move to the secondary and finally address the tertiary objectives.

The primary objectives represent the starting points for immediate action. The secondary objectives show the sequence of objectives that may be added if you have time and capacity after starting/completing your primary objectives. Likewise, the tertiary objectives show the sequence of objectives that you should initiate once you have capacity amidst or after implementing the primary and secondary objectives. I recommend handling the objectives in this fashion so that you see returns immediately, do not burn yourself out and do not hurt your inner circle or close group relationships (Figure 3). If you followed the process, an example for the sorted list of objectives is tabulated in **Table 3.**

Table 3 - Sorted list of prioritized objectives

Objective Level	Objective	Relative Score %
Ob-1	Happy family life	22%
Ob-5	Build business and technical relevant expertise	19%
Ob-2	Financially free by 45	18%
Ob-4	Adopt a healthy lifestyle	17%
Ob-3	Travel locally and abroad	14%
Ob-7	Career development to company head	10%
Ob-6	Develop specialist technical and business qualifications	0%
Ob-8	Mulitple income sources and financial freedom	0%

Table 3 shows that objectives Ob-1 and Ob-5 are the primary objectives. Objectives Ob-2, Ob-4 and Ob-3 are the secondary objectives. Objectives Ob-7, Ob-6 and Ob-8 are the tertiary objectives. This shows a focus on personal life improvement as well as effort that will help your professional life. Once the goals associated with Ob-1 and Ob-5 are implemented/started and you find that you have capacity, the goals associated with objective Ob-2 then Ob-4 may be started. As explained above, as you generate capacity, start with the next goal or next objective and its set of goals. If this excites you, then you prioritized properly. If not, rethink fast because this is going to be your life for the next many years and I suggest that you choose to be happy and motivated instead of grumpy and irritated.

At this stage, it will be good to discuss this plan with your spouse and/or significant other(s) to make sure that they understand your actions for the near future. The idea is to build a better version of yourself that enables you to make effective decisions for your life to get you to your definition of success. It is certainly NOT to be used as a reason or means to break significant relationships. Make no mistake, embarking on this journey will have an impact on all of your relationships, but it is important to contextualize each relationship and its value to you – use Figure 3, the Circles of Influence. If any of those relationships are not where they should be in your life, this exercise demonstrates that you should consider how to strengthen or adjust the respective relationship(s) as part of your goals. In doing so, you will address obstacles along your journey. My view is that (immediate) family always comes first so be sure to protect these relationships.

Back to the plan, before you marvel at your life choices for the short-, medium- and long-term, consider that you only have direction at this stage and no path. That comes next so do not put your pen and paper/book away just yet because it's time to script your path to success.

Establishing Goals – The Path to Achieving the Objectives

This is one of the exciting parts of the process because this is where the picture of how you are going to realize your vision of success starts to become clearer with each input and/or iteration. To explain this, your goals are meant to describe how you will achieve each objective. In the hierarchy of the plan, the life plan depends on the PDP and the PrDP, the PDP and the PrDP are described by objectives and each objective is described by multiple goals, see **Figure 11.**

Figure 11 - Life Plan Hierarchy and Relationship

Figure 11 shows the hierarchy and relationship among the goals, objectives, PDP, PrDP and life plan. The life plan exists at the highest level and represents your vision. The PDP and PrDP represent the "strategic level", which is corporate lingo for your plan to realize your vision. Your objectives will provide direction on how your strategy will be delivered – in other words, it is your mission through your objectives. Your goals represent the consolidation of all your tasks and actions as these feed into their respective objective(s).

Goals are meant to be tangible, clear, quantifiable and measurable (yes, there is a difference between quantify and measure). "Quantify" talks to the importance of the goal and "measure" relates to the influence that achieving that goal has on your success story. Delivering your goals (through your actions and tasks) will determine how close you are to getting on track with your preferred direction and how far you are from your vision of success through your PDP and PrDP.

When I did this, my process was riddled with confusion because I mixed my goals and objectives. I addressed this confusion by ensuring that each goal was measurable and quantifiable as a minimum. I described my objectives to be intangible and unmeasurable on their own. For example, a goal for me was to qualify with my MBA degree by age 50. The quantity was the (one) MBA degree and the measure being "by age 50". This aligned with my PrDP objective to "develop specialist technical and business qualifications" (Ob-6) and my PDP objective to "build business and technical relevant expertise" (Ob-5). You will see that I cannot measure Ob-5 and Ob-6 on their own, I need to achieve the goals associated with Ob-5 and Ob-6 to be able to measure my progress with each objective. Therefore, I can only measure and describe Ob-5 and Ob-6 through measuring the progress of the goals associated with each. In this way you manage your life plan at a single level and those actions roll up to give you progress and results towards your objectives, PDP, PrDP and life plan. It makes sense, therefore, to ensure that you describe your goals associated with each objective really well.

Be cautious not to be too detailed and establish too many goals. I made this mistake with my PDP and quickly rationalised my goals to something manageable, easy to quantify and measure, but offered a strong challenge to achieve. After doing this rationalization, I found that I was more productive with my life plan, family and work.

To establish your goals, recall your brainstorming and rationalizing exercises. These are a good starting point because these offer early insight towards your goals and are a good platform to start planning your goals. This may be confusing and I am sure that there will be multiple views on how to complete this part of the exercise. To make sure that we remain on the same wavelength, the next few paragraphs explain the process that I followed.

Take for example objective Ob-1 "Happy family life", the brainstorming and rationalizing exercise showed that having "3 children by age 32" and "visiting a different family member every weekend" were important aspects raised. But these may be insufficient goals because some aspect may be missing. Remember that until now you did this exercise on your own because you needed to be clear to yourself about the personal and professional objectives that would make you happy with a sense of fulfilment. It is safe to invite trusted members from your inner circle and perhaps the Close Group into the planning. These are the group of people that know you better than most people and would be interested in seeing you progress (we hope). If not, time to get a new set of members in the two main circles.

Let's assume that the engagement was great and after consolidating all feedback you were able to add three more goals to what would contribute to a "Happy family life". Remember that each goal must be tangible, quantifiable and measurable. Complex goals must be able to be measured through some sort of progress and simple goals will be binary – either it's done or it's not. A complex goal will be, for example, studying the MBA degree because there are many parts to it and you will experience value after you complete each module. While the degree is important, you may need a few modules (e.g. finance, strategy and process & systems) to achieve what you require from this goal for your objective. In this case, the MBA degree offers a formal qualification with more value than you actually require. Completing the degree allows you the benefit of the knowledge from the three modules identified, knowledge from other modules that will benefit you and the formal qualification. If you don't complete the MBA degree for whatever reason, you will have gained the knowledge from the three important modules and will therefore not need to amend your plan. On the downside, you will not have achieved the qualification benefit. If your plan is clear that you want the MBA degree as well, then only part of your objective will be met until you complete the degree. Only once you complete the MBA degree will you be able to achieve the full benefit of the knowledge and the qualification.

A simple goal requires all aspects to be completed before you receive the value from that goal. The goal for "3 children by age 32" will be a simple goal because only once you have your three children will you be satisfied with this goal. Anything children less will mean that this goal was not achieved, or you need to amend your plan at some future state.

Again, give yourself the best chance for success by ensuring that your energy is allocated beneficially among the goals. I found that assigning each goal a score out of 100 and no duplicate scores, as was done when prioritizing the objectives, gave me good direction to allocating my time and energy. Now assign each goal a label related to their specific objective, e.g. Ob-1, so that you can track where your energy is being expended. I used my corporate and engineering experiences for each label and came up with G-1-01 that will be translated to goal (G) tied to objective Ob-1 (-1) and it is the first goal for that objective (-01). The value of labelling is that it gives you simpler descriptions so that you don't have to constantly refer to your workings to understand each objective and goal pair. As before, find what works for you then decide where you will get the most benefit and give that goal the highest score, as illustrated in **Figure 12**. Please keep it simple, you are not trying to impress anybody. You are targeting to express yourself to achieve your vision of success.

Figure 12 - Qualified goals for prioritized objectives

Figure 12 shows that for objective Ob-1, the immediate action will be directed towards having a family (30%) followed by visiting family (25%), new goal1 (19%), new goal2 (14%) and then new goal 3 (12%). You now have a path to achieving objective Ob-1 through the five goals. Once all goals are achieved, the objective will have been achieved and you would be 21% closer to your vision of success (see **Table 2** where you assigned objective Ob-1 a score of 21/100 = 21%).

Recall the distinction between goals and objectives using **Figure 12**. Objective Ob-1 cannot be measured for progress or value on its own, but by measuring the progress or value from each goal that describes Ob-1, you will be able to calculate the progress for Ob-1.

What's left is to split each goal into discreet actions and tasks that are tangible and will deliver the goal once completed. This will be a personal exercise and depends on your views of the actions to meet each goal and the level of detail that you want to develop. As a hint, I recommend an order of precedence as goal→task→action, meaning that the goal is higher than task, which is higher than actions. Once you have done this, remember the conundrum of where to start. This will be easily addressed by assigning priorities to each task that describes a goal such that all tasks that describe a particular goal totals 100%. The same can be done for actions, should you choose to go to that level of detail. Be cautious not to expend time developing too detailed a plan that will be an administrative nightmare. The goal (excuse the pun) is to get you to your vision of success and not boggled with administration. It will be key to be functional and practical to achieve this. I used a hybrid approach where some goals needed expanding because these were complex goals, but most of my goals were simple goals and did not need to go to the task or action level.

It is a given in life that there are no free lunches. This means that among your goals should be the means to secure the funding that you need. This could be loans, savings, proceeds from investments, sale of goods (refrain from selling your home and its contents), bursaries, scholarships and possibly internships. Note, inheritance, gambling and prayer are not sources of funding – these are long term hopes and will never materialise in time (if at all) to be of value to you when you need it. If things work out for you this way, then well done and I hope that you make the most of your good fortune.

Repeat this exercise for all identified objectives and you will have established your path to success through your personal and professional life. This might sound too detailed and mathematical, but this is only a once off exercise. Once you set the goals, you will have defined your tasks and actions for the foreseeable future – so please persevere.

My Life Plan

When I reached this stage, I was quite satisfied with what I had developed for myself – albeit over many years. In order to avoid wasted effort by taking the wrong action from any of the work done, there needed to be distinction around the development work and the actual product to take action. Achieving this meant that there had to be discreet processes where each activity could be categorized and recorded, which led to what I term as the "3-Page Exercise" and "My Life Plan".

The effort to define what I wanted and how I was going to get what I wanted was important and could be integrated into a single exercise. This is termed "My 3-Page Exercise", comprising:

- Brainstorming.
- Rationalizing.
- Prioritizing my plan.

The 3-Page Exercise meant multiple outputs that could become onerous to manage. The elements of the 3-Page Exercise were developed as building blocks, meaning that each progressive output was an elaboration of the previous deliverable. That is, the brainstorming exercises build up to the rationalized plans, which build up to the prioritized plans. On their own, this meant managing a PDP and the PrDP separately, which I considered to be an area for potential time and resource wastage. Combining the PDP and PrDP into a single plan, being My Life Plan, made sense because this brought all goals and objectives together as a single deliverable. Once done, the life plan illustrated a clear path for me to break through my glass ceiling and address the matters important to me. For me, developing the 3-Page Plan and My Life Plan aims to convert dreams into goals, goals into tasks and actions to guide where time and money should be spent to achieve my vision of success.

I often got to the stage of thinking that I may have become too theoretical, which led to me slipping from the process for a while. Fortunately, I returned to the exercise shortly after slipping and managed to complete the next bit. I was pleasantly surprised with how the prioritization exercise clarified my objectives through the interests-importance matrix. The plan demonstrated how I could focus my energy and make decisions for my best interest – and for my family's best interest because this was a key element for me.

After analysing my life plan, there were other objectives and goals that I was tempted to add to the plan, but when I analysed these, it was clear to me that those were not adding value to my vision of success. While I didn't want to admit it, the plan showed that there were a number of activities that I undertook where I received no value and some where I was moving away from my vision of success. This gave me the platform to be critical to myself and make important decisions on my behaviours going forward.

Developing my life plan was daunting for me and consumed a large part of my free time. My first plan, after my 1992 revelation, took approximately seven weeks (if memory serves me correct). My final life plan, after my 2004 revelation, was more functional plan and took approximately five months to build. Your timeline will depend on the effort and commitment that you place on your vision of success.

One of the benefits of the process is that you don't have to wait for the final product(s) before taking urgent action. I found that the prioritized PDP and PrDP were sufficient for decision making concerning immediate opportunities that arose where value would be delivered to me. Conversely, I was able to separate opportunities that looked good (or popular) from those that were good. This was beneficial because by rejecting those opportunities, I had sufficient time and resources to take advantage of the important opportunities that would get me closer to my vision of success. Hopefully you learn from my lessons and get to a functional plan in the shortest time.

To accelerate your anticipation (and motivate you to push through the exercise), find attached part of my life plan (details removed of course) in **Figure 13.**

My life Plan

My Personal Development Plan (PDP) - Continued on next page

Objective OB-1 (22%) Happy Family Life	Objective OB-2 (18%) Financially free by 45	Objective OB-3 (14%) Travel local and abroad	Objective OB-4 (17%) Healthy lifestyle
Goal 1: G-1-01 (30%) 3 kids by age 32	Goal 1: G-2-01 (18%) Pay bond by 45	Goal 1: G-3-01 (18%) Holiday every 3 months	Goal 1: G-4-01 (18%) Lose weight in 8 months to goal weight
Goal 2: G-1-02 (25%) Visit family members on weekends	Goal 2: G-2-02 (25%) Multiple income sources	Goal 2: G-3-02 (25%) International holiday every year	Goal 2: G-4-02 (25%) Start gym training 5 times/week, in 2 weeks
Goal 3: G-1-03 (19%) New goal 1	Goal 3: G-2-03 (15%) Rental property in 3 countries	Goal 3: G-3-03 (19%) New goal 1	Goal 3: G-4-03 (19%) Take frequent local holidays/breakaways
Goal 4: G-1-04 (14%) New goal 2	Goal 4: G-2-04 (14%) New goal 1	Goal 4: G-3-04 (14%) New goal 2	Goal 4: G-4-04 (14%) New goal 1
Goal 5: G-1-0 (12%) New goal 3	Goal 5: G-2-05 (12%) New goal 2	Goal 5: G-3-05 (12%) New goal 3	Goal 5: G-4-05 (12%) New goal 2

Figure 13 - Example of a life plan

Figure 13 shows excerpts of my life plan to take me towards my vision of success. The plan is visual, simple and in a format that synchronises with the brain. An important point to note is that the plan is a good guide for all decisions, so you must bring your spouse or significant other(s) into the process. Their support will be invaluable through your journey but you will also likely inspire them to do something similar and possibly embark on this journey together. This will play a role in strengthening some of the most important relationships in your life so make sure that you are ready for the challenge.

Analysing **Figure 13** shows a few key points that must be discussed. The glaring aspect is the focus and perceived priorities. It is clear that there is a stronger focus on personal development, family and health. The professional development milestone is geared towards career growth and links with the personal growth. This is good because it shows that there are some goals that will satisfy parts of the personal and professional life simultaneously – saving time, money and offering earlier satisfaction.

The goals specific to objective Ob-2 will materially influence your professional life through objective Ob-8. Do not be tempted to assign a priority to Ob-8 because this is not about progress but about growth. Assigning a progress will skew your focus and will offer little benefit. By assigning the higher priority to Ob-2, you will address Ob-8 and Ob-2. You will note then that the goals for Ob-8 have been illustrated under Ob-2 thereby demonstrating the synergy that may be achieved after applying diligence and effort. The same applies for objectives Ob-5 and Ob-6.

There are situations where an objective appears to be a goal to another objective – see objective Ob-5 as a goal (G-7-05, Figure 13) to objective Ob-7. This is acceptable and again shows synergy. Additionally, it also shows that objective Ob-7 has more goals that need to be satisfied before realising that objective. Don't stress about delay or missing professional opportunities because your plan demonstrates how you will generate more value by focusing on the right elements that are tied to a big picture. In corporate terms, objectives ties to a strategy to realise your vision. This will shape your mission, being your present action(s).

Keep in mind that if your definition of what you want doesn't scare you, you're not thinking big enough.

Increasing the Life Plan's Utility

To recap, you discovered more about yourself and what you want; you converted that into prioritized objectives that would deliver your version of a successful life and you distilled the objectives into multiple goals – with their priorities. Sounds simple, but do not underestimate the effort and thought that was required to get here – it is tremendous! The big question at this stage – before operationalising the plan – is: have you achieved maximum utility from the plan?

As is, the plan will be sufficient to guide your decisions and actions. For the more detailed oriented reader, there is an additional technique that can be used to increase the plans utility and is as simple as mapping. Mapping will show various linkages among the goals and also provide insight into where you may benefit from synergies among goals for best value returns. An example of a mapped life plan is illustrated in **Figure 14**. The colour of the arrows is only to show forward or reverse linkage to avoid confusion.

Primary Objective
Secondary Objective
Tertiary Objective

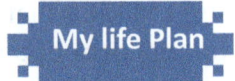
My life Plan

My Personal Development Plan (PDP) - Continued on the next page

Objective OB-1 (22%) Happy Family Life	Objective OB-2 (18%) Financially free by 45	Objective OB-3 (14%) Travel local and abroad	Objective OB-4 (17%) Healthy lifestyle
Goal 1: G-1-01 (30%) 3 kids by age 32	Goal 1: G-2-01 (18%) Pay bond by 45	Goal 1: G-3-01 (18%) Holiday every 3 months	Goal 1: G-4-01 (18%) Lose weight in 8 months to goal weight
Goal 2: G-1-02 (25%) Visit family members on weekends	Goal 2: G-2-02 (25%) Multiple income sources	Goal 2: G-3-02 (25%) International holiday every year	Goal 2: G-4-02 (25%) Start gym training 5 times/week, in 2 weeks
Goal 3: G-1-03 (19%) New goal 1	Goal 3: G-2-03 (15%) Rental property in 3 countries	Goal 3: G-3-03 (19%) New goal 1	Goal 3: G-4-03 (19%) Take frequent local holidays/ breakaways
Goal 4: G-1-04 (14%) New goal 2	Goal 4: G-2-04 (14%) New goal 1	Goal 4: G-3-04 (14%) New goal 2	Goal 4: G-4-04 (14%) New goal 1
Goal 5: G-1-0 (12%) New goal 3	Goal 5: G-2-05 (12%) New goal 2	Goal 5: G-3-05 (12%) New goal 3	Goal 5: G-4-05 (12%) New goal 2

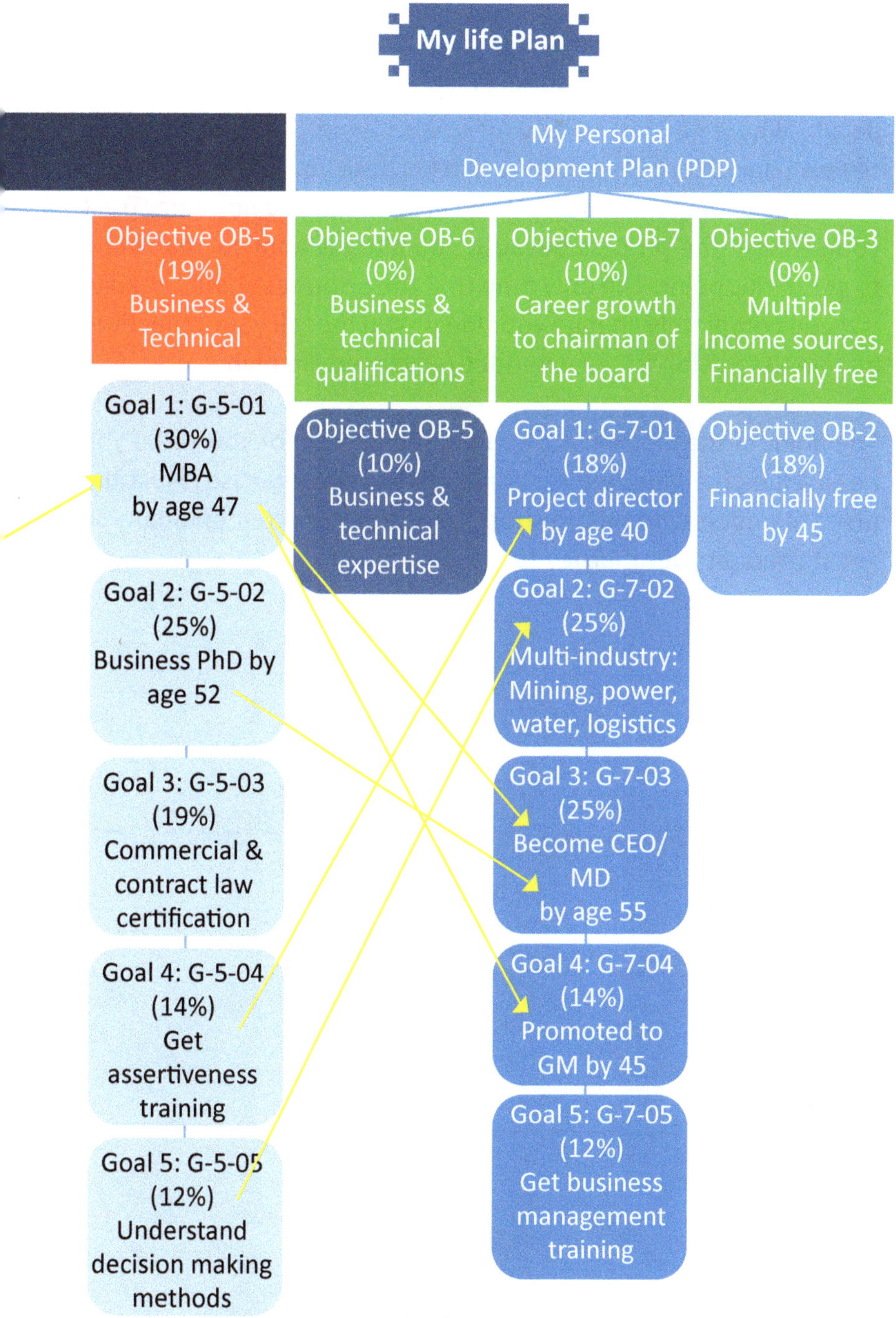

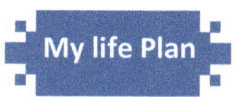

Figure 14 - Example of prioritized and linked life plan

Figure 14 shows that while you start with your primary objectives, your action on some goals will influence and add value to your secondary and/or tertiary objectives. This will also help you to decide where to start with your goals. Avoid the temptation to review your objectives prioritization because you will find yourself in a never-ending loop that will end in lost time and no value. Trust yourself and the process because you already applied your mind to get to this point. The only time that the priorities should change is if you completely change your life or you met all your objectives and need to establish an extended/advanced life plan.

The point of the life plan is also to contextualise for yourself if you need a life-changing re-direction. Part 1 of this exercise is just the place to understand this. In short, this exercise is your epiphany so get started on your journey to a successful life.

Bringing it All Together – The 3-Page Plan

The life plan provided excellent context to take measured and focussed action towards my vision of success. Each goal and objective achieved meant that I would have experienced growth in my personal life, professional life or both. For me, it was important to assess the impact of the growth to myself holistically by being able to assess if I was getting what I wanted and how this shaped me as a person. To achieve this, I brought the three key deliverables together into what I called my 3-Page plan that reminded me who I was, what I wanted and how I was going to get what I wanted. To simplify, the 3-Page Plan content is described below and illustrated in **Figure 15**

- Page 1: Who am I? See Table 1 - Example of results for a self-reflection exercise (Step 1).
- Page 2: What do I want? See Table 2 - Table of Prioritized Objectives (Step 2).
- Page 3: My Life Plan, see Figure 13 - Example of a Life Plan (result of Steps 3 to 5). I prefer to use **Figure 14 - Example of prioritized and linked life plan** because it shows the integration.

Figure 15 demonstrates that the 3-Page plan is a consolidated reminder of where you are versus where you want to be and how you are going to reach your destination. You will be able to store your other works away and avoid having to switch through multiple cumbersome documents while still gaining the value from what you built for yourself. If you build your 3-Page plan, you will be able to keep the three pages with you at all times or post the three pages on your wall as a constant visual reminder of everything that you want and want to become. Page 2 of the 3-Page Plan can include the PDP and PrDP as independent objectives with **Table 2.**

After developing my first 3-Page Plan, my first question was how was I going to afford this? When I looked at my 3-Page plan, I did identify sources of funds (yes – salary, investments and supplemental business were among the sources) for certain goals, which proved to me that I had done a good job of describing my goals and objectives. Note the choice of words, "good" not "perfect" or "best". Life happened along my journey and while certain sources of funding worked, most didn't. My goals remained and I needed the funds to support some objectives, meaning that my life plan did not have to change, it needed minor tweaks.

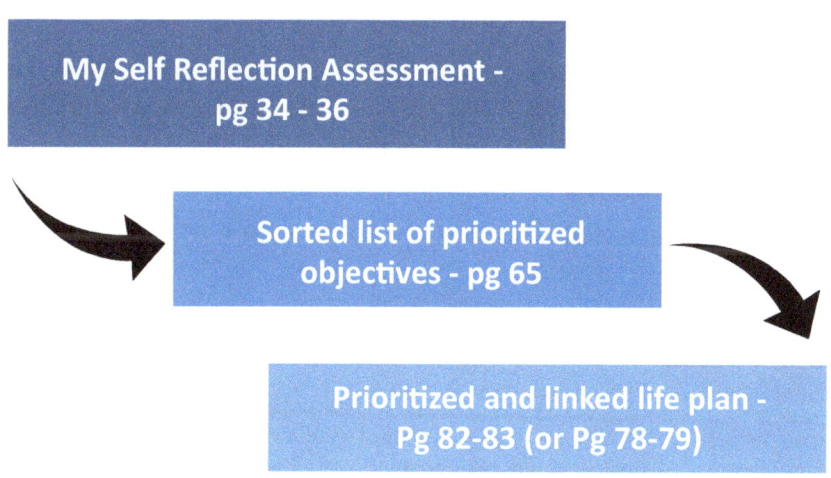

Figure 15 - The 3-page plan to Achieve Your Vision of Success

Measuring and Monitoring Your Performance

There will always be those among us that may choose to avoid measuring and monitoring for various reasons. Some of the reasons that I heard were that this is a theoretical exercise, it can be too academic with no real applicability, it increases administration, it requires too much time to address and that it is intimidating because math is not their strong point.

The good news is that measuring and monitoring can be made as simple or as complicated as you want. Some keep measuring and monitoring simple so that they may always have a handle over its utility. Most people choose the complicated route because they have a good grasp of electronic tools and software and can develop the required programs. Others may like the pictures that the data allows to be generated, while some may want to impress people around them with their tools and progress gained.

Let me share that I've never seen value in trying to impress people, but saw exceptional value in expressing myself to the best of my ability. I find no value in living my life to other people's standards and other people's terms. My view is that we will never be able to please everybody but run the real risk of losing our identity while trying to impress others. I observed many instances when this happened and noted how people lost the respect of the person that they were trying to impress because they were "too needy" – actual response that I overheard several times.

Whichever route you choose, I implore you to adopt some kind of measuring and monitoring for your life plan. If you choose to omit measuring and monitoring from your process, all good to you. Before you finalize this choice, please consider my thoughts below where I hope to convince you otherwise.

To simplify this part of the process, I split this section into three parts, namely:

- The value of measuring and monitoring.
- Overview to measuring and monitoring.
- Detailed measuring and monitoring process.

The Value of Measuring and Monitoring

As a project manager I cannot overstate the value of measuring and monitoring to any endeavour that you choose to undertake. This is especially useful when you expect returns and when the stakes are as high as your vision of success. Contrary to most beliefs, measuring and monitoring is not meant to be punitive or complicated, but a means to identify risks and opportunities early to allow best chance for success.

Despite being used predominantly in the corporate world, measuring and monitoring is another corporate tool that has equal applicability to our personal life. Relating to your life plan, since you defined what success looks like for you, each action you take will either get you closer to your vision of success, take you further away from your vision of success or offer no benefit to you to reach your vision of success. If you are able to understand and measure the impact of each action, you will be in the best position to implement some action to improve your situation.

I often encountered the retort that if something is not broken, there is no need to fix it. My response is very simple on this matter – how do you know if something is broken or not? I heard many different responses to that question, but the simple fact is that one only knows if something is broken when that something stops working. Others choose to consistently assess outputs to determine if production is being hampered, while some wait for symptoms to appear then treat the symptoms. Here is the bad news – all of the above are measuring and monitoring techniques. Some are more sophisticated than others and some are binary (works or does not work). Semantics are not going to help you get to where you want to be; but will see that you waste valuable time arguing a moot point. Let's call a "spade a spade" and agree that you will be doing some form of progress tracking for most things that you do, but the level of sophistication will vary. Your life plan is no different. Even if you think there are no results or benefits, this effectively is a zero-value result, meaning that you are doing unconscious measuring and monitoring.

Returning to the point, the benefit of implementing a measuring and monitoring component to your life plan is that you will have a baseline to compare your perceived benefit or loss. The baseline comparison will indicate where you are detracting from your purpose and where action is needed to restore, turnaround (change) or accelerate certain actions.

Note: *I distinguish between reaction and response because I consider reaction to be exactly what the word says: action to some stimulus. Response, for me, is measured and considered action to an event to deliver a higher purpose.*

Effective measuring and monitoring will instil proactive behaviour with your life plan so that you reap maximum benefit. The method can get involved and become too mathematical, which I often find is a put-off to most people. To pull all readers along the same journey, the overview below offers a high-level approach and the detailed measurement plan gives you a more in-depth approach. All readers will gain similar value from the book through the overview. The detailed measurement plan is an extension to the overview and will take readers who choose to implement a quantifiable measurement plan through a step-by-step process.

Measurement and Monitoring Overview

The elevator pitch for measuring and monitoring is to identify whether your actions are delivering value or not. The simplest way to do this is to check how many goals you have associated with each objective and used the goal description to assess if you made progress or not. If you did what the goal said, then you are closer to competing the objective. As you complete all goals, your objective will be achieved. This method is simple and may be monitored by simply ticking off the goal on your life plan, **Figure 14 - Example of prioritized and linked life plan.** As you tick off goals, you will see how close each objective is from completion and therefore how far you are from completing your PDP and PrDP.

A value-add of measuring and monitoring is that it allows you to assess, take stock and direct or re-direct. After taking stock, you will understand better if your defined goals are aligned to its respective objective. If the goal is aligned, you will start to experience some of the benefit from that goal-objective pairing and you may continue (or direct) with your defined actions. If not, your goals must be amended (re-direct) such that these amended goal(s) will be better aligned to achieving a respective objective.

If you need to re-direct, do not despair because you are not alone. I had to re-direct a few times and I am sure that many who follow this approach (or any other similar approach) will have to re-direct at various stages as well. Re-directing simply means that you need more information and support to help you on your journey. I often found that turning to my inner and trusted circles for feedback were most beneficial when re-directing.

The Detailed Measuring and Monitoring Plan

For the readers that want to take up the detailed challenge, brace yourself for a mathematical adventure. I included examples to stimulate your creative mind and channel that energy to make sense for you.

The process starts with defining a common set of milestones that you believe would describe the various stages of progress as you reach your goal. An example of simple milestones for each goal could be:

- Milestone 1: I know what to do (10%).
- Milestone 2: I started with the actions and tasks (70%).
- Milestone 3: I completed the goal (20%).

The milestones should be broken into tangible actions from planning to implementation and should include a perceived value gained/expected from each milestone – must total 100%. Once you have done this, you will have described what you need to do to achieve your goals and by inference, your objective(s). As you achieve each objective, you will gain progress against the PDP and the PrDP, which in-turn, will give you indication of the value that you gained towards your vision of success.

Actions/tasks that are tangible makes the outcome of your actions binary, that is, either you completed the action/task or did not. If you completed the action/task, you will have got closer to your goal; if you did not complete the action/task, you will have not achieved the goal and will not enjoy the full benefit that you deemed that goal would offer to you. For the milestone examples indicated above, once you defined what needs to be done, you will have completed Milestone 1 and achieved 10% progress towards that goal. If you started with the actions related to a goal and finished half of what you planned to do for that goal, then you achieved half the progress for that milestone, which is 50% of 70% = 35% for Milestone 2. Since you did not finish Milestones 2 and 3, you will not get the progress associated with Milestone 3 and will not get the remaining progress from Milestone 2. In this case, because of the work you did towards that goal, your progress on the goal from Milestones 1, 2 and 3 will be: 10% + 35% + 0% = 45%. Remember that you must complete a task to get the progress so do not complicate your life by trying to measure each task individually – keep it simple. Be mindful that the plan will take time to materialize. Do not be swayed if your progress is slow because it is more important that you are moving forward and making progress. As you get more involved with the plan you will build momentum which will accelerate your progress.

Now for the confusing bit. I found that more milestones helped to motivate me because I could measure my performance regularly. Small actions that I completed for each goal could be measured and I experienced its benefits early. Therefore, when I set-up my monitoring and measuring tool, I expanded Milestones 1, 2 and 3 from the example above into more milestones that I believed would better describe my progress to completion. Table 4 identifies the milestones that I used for measuring and monitoring my life plan.

Table 4 - Possible measuring and monitoring milestones

Item	Milestone Description	Milestone Progress
1	Scope identified	3%
2	Timeline identified	2%
3	Started with actions	5%
4	Actions complete	35%
5	Benefits realised	15%
6	Satisfied with outcome	40%
	Total of weighted scoring	100%

Table 4 summarizes the milestones with their respective weights to describe the progress for each goal. As described above, the milestone progress measures are weighted measures that is set once for the life of your life plan. If you do change these values, it is at your discretion and will make life unnecessarily complicated, so take time and define the milestones properly. Milestone 4, Actions Complete, refers to carrying out each item that you identify that is needed for each goal. I've applied this approach as a project manager and experienced great value that allowed proactive response.

Before going further, let's contextualise the process in line with Stephen Covey's principle of "begin with the end in mind" as the starting point. Your Life Plan comprises two elements, your PDP and PrDP, which were each broken into multiple objectives through the brainstorming activity. The objectives were prioritised, **Table 2**, and categorised into the PDP and PrDP. From **Table 2**, objectives Ob-1-5 are categorised as PDP objectives and if their priority scores are added, this totals 90%. This means that once you achieve all objectives for the PDP, you will have gained 100%

benefit from the PDP, but a maximum of 90% benefit envisaged for your success story through your life plan. Recall that the PDP carries 90% weighting towards the life plan, thus the value gained from the PDP towards your success story will be 100% of 90% = 90%. At this point, you will be able to assess if that value and its benefits are real. So too, if you completed objective Ob2 only, you would have achieved 18% of the benefit to the Life Plan and 20% (18% ÷ 90%) of the benefit from your PDP. The same principle applies to the PrDP in relation to the Life Plan and value to you. To make life simpler so that you can focus your attention where it belongs, take this information and commit it to a simple table, as illustrated in **Table 5**.

Table 5 - Proposed milestone and progress monitoring

Life Plan Progress			
Personal Development Plan (PDP) Progress			
Objective	Relative Weight	Weighted Average Objective Progress	Weighted Average PDP Progress
Ob-1	22%		
Ob-2	18%		
Ob-3	14%		
Ob-4	17%		
Ob-5	19%		

Life Plan Progress			
Professional Development Plan (PrDP) Progress			
Objective	Relative Weight	Weighted Average Objective Progress	Weighted Average PDP Progress
Ob-6	0%		
Ob-7	10%		
Ob-8	0%		

From **Table 5**, the "Relative Weight" is the priority that was set earlier. The "Weighted Average Objective Progress" will be the progress that the objective experiences as each goal is delivered and will be a maximum value equal to the relative weight (or priority) set. The "Weighted Average PDP/PrDP Progress" refers to the progress that the objective will deliver to the PDP/PrDP as the objective is being delivered through its goals. The next key step is to define the goals, its link to the objectives and how it will influence the PDP and PrDP.

If you believe, e.g. goal 2 for objective 4 has four tasks, then each task is recorded with six milestones described above. Each of the four tasks will have their own percentage weight that will describe how much progress each contributes to that goal. The goal, in turn, has its own weighted percentage progress that describes how much progress that goal will contribute to its respective objective. Once you have reached this level of definition, you are ready to start measuring your progress.

The next question will naturally be "how" to measure progress of the actions and/or tasks that will feed up to the goals and further. For this, use **Table 4** and apply those milestones to each task and/or action. You can choose the level of detail that you prefer to adopt, but I recommend the task level. An example of this is illustrated in **Table 6 and Table 7. Table 6 shows the overall table with reference to the progress milestones that are expanded in Table 7. Therefore, your table should be a single table where the content from Table 7 are included in Table 6 from the beginning.**

Table 6 - Example of tasks (or actions) linked to goals and objectives for measuring progress

Table 6 - Progress measurement

Label	Descirption	Goal Weight	Objective
G-1-01	3 kids by age 32	30%	1
G-1-02	Visit family members on weekends	25%	1
G-1-03	New goal 1	45%	1
G-2-01	Pay bond by 45	18%	2
G-2-02	Multiple income sources	25%	2
G-2-03	Rental property in 3 countries	57%	2
G-3-01	Holiday every 3 months	18%	3
G-3-02	International holiday every year	25%	3
G-3-03	New goal 1	57%	3
G-4-01	Lose weight in 8 months to goal weight	18%	4
G-4-02	Start gym training 5 times/week	82%	4
G-5-01	MBA by age 47	30%	5
G-5-02	Business PhD by 52	25%	5
G-5-03	Commercial & contact Law certification	19%	5
G-5-04	Get Assertiveness training	26%	5
G-6-01	MBA by age 47	30%	6
G-6-02	Business PhD by age 52	70%	6
G-7-01	Project director by age 40	18%	7
G-7-02	Multi-industry: mining, power, water, logistics	25%	7
G-7-03	Become CEO/MD by age 55	19%	7
G-7-04	Promoted to GM by age 45	38%	7
G-8-01	Pay bond by 45	18%	8
G-8-02	Multiple income sources	82%	8

Progress Milestones	Average Goal Progress	Weighted Average Goal Progress	Weighted Average Objective Progress
	0%	0%	0%
	0%	0%	
	0%	0%	
	0%	0%	0%
	0%	0%	
	0%	0%	
	0%	0%	0%
	0%	0%	
	0%	0%	
	0%	0%	0%
	0%	0%	
	0%	0%	0%
	0%	0%	
	0%	0%	
	0%	0%	
	0%	0%	0%
	0%	0%	
	0%	0%	0%
	0%	0%	
	0%	0%	
	0%	0%	
	0%	0%	0%
	0%	0%	

*Progress Milestones are expanded in the next table, but should be included with this table when developing.

Table 7 - Progress measurement

Label	Descirption	Scope Identified	Timeline Finalised
		3%	2%
G-1-01	3 kids by age 32		
G-1-02	Visit family members on weekends		
G-1-03	New goal 1		
G-2-01	Pay bond by 45		
G-2-02	Multiple income sources		
G-2-03	Rental property in 3 countries		
G-3-01	Holiday every 3 months		
G-3-02	International holiday every year		
G-3-03	New goal 1		
G-4-01	Lose weight in 8 months to goal weight		
G-4-02	Start gym training 5 times/week		
G-5-01	MBA by age 47		
G-5-02	Business PhD by 52		
G-5-03	Commercial & contact Law certification		
G-5-04	Get Assertiveness training		
G-6-01	MBA by age 47		
G-6-02	Business PhD by age 52		
G-7-01	Project director by age 40		
G-7-02	Multi-industry: mining, power, water, logistics		
G-7-03	Become CEO/MD by age 55		
G-7-04	Promoted to GM by age 45		
G-8-01	Pay bond by 45		
G-8-02	Multiple income sources		

	Started with actions	Actions complete	Benefits realised	Satisfied with outcome
	5%	35%	15%	40%

Table 6 and Table 7 shows that all goals are linked to objectives and has its associated progress measurement with weightings. Adopt the same approach if you choose to go into the task and action level of detail, but recall the precedence discussed above – actions feed up to tasks and tasks feed up into goals. For this book, the goals level is preferred as the lowest level of detail.

If you followed the linkages described above, you will see that you only need to update the progress at your lowest level of definition – for this book that is the goals level. As you update the progress at the goals level (or your defined lowest level), the calculation through the described linkages will carry to the objectives level, the PDP/PrDP level and ultimately the Life Plan level – that's working smart.

To illustrate how this will work, let us simulate the progress measurement using Table 4 for goal G-1-01 to have "3 kids by age 32" (for example). If you identified the scope (tasks and actions) for G-1-01, you can claim 100% complete and that will mean that you will have achieved the 3% relative progress associated with goal G-1-01. If you confirmed and finalised the timeline that you want for goal G-1-01, that milestone will also be 100% complete and you will have earned an additional 2% progress for goal G-1-01. At this point, your total progress for the goal will be 5% (2% + 3%). If you started with your actions, then that milestone is 100% completed, you will have gained additional 5% progress and your overall progress for G-1-01 will be 10% (2% + 3% + 5%). If your tasks and/or actions associated with G-1-01 are 50% completed, then the "Actions complete" milestone progress will be 50%, you will have gained additional 50% of 35% = 17.5% progress towards G-1-01, and your total progress will be 27.5% (2% + 3% + 5% + 17.5%) for goal G-1-01. At this point, because goal G-1-01 was weighted as 30% contribution to objective Ob-1, after completing the above for G-1-01, G-1-01's 27.5% progress will have delivered

8.3% (27.5% of 30%) progress to objective Ob-1. If the other two goals (G-1-02 and G-1-03) have not been progressed, this means that objective Ob-1 will have achieved 8.3% progress in total. Extending this further, objective Ob-1 was rated at 22% value to the PDP, meaning that the PDP will have gained 1.8% (8.3% of 22%) from the effort delivered to goal G-1-01. For the purpose of this example, we will take the PrDP goals progress as 0, meaning that you will have achieved 1.8% progress (or value) to your success story through your life plan.

Moving away from the math, you will notice that for this goal, 50% achievement could mean one and a half children. This is impractical to measure and will be even more fruitless to try to find the means to assess exact progress. Developing your plan will see that you identify and cut out the background noise through focused thought and considered action. This applies to progress measurement because semantics and overly detailed methods will create unnecessary distractions. In this case, having decided to have "3 kids" will offer 100% achievement on the "scope identified" milestone; "by age 32" gives 100% achievement on the "timeline identified milestone" while starting to take action to have kids (the traditional route and/or adoption) will provide 100% achievement on the "started with actions" milestone. Upon taking all actions, you will have achieved progress against the "actions complete" milestone. In the case of having children, there will be repeat actions needed for each child so my recommendation would be to take this milestone to 75% for your first child, then 90% when you have your second child and finally 100% when you have your third child. Once you have your first child, that will mean 33.3% achievement against the "benefits realised" milestone. This is an example of a complex goal because having your first child will give progress against the "actions complete" milestone and to the "benefits realised" milestone without first achieving 100% against the "actions complete" milestone. This is perfectly acceptable because this is how the process accommodates for life's uncertainties to ensure that you always have a plan to move forward and grow.

There is another part that can get tricky. If you decide that you want to stop after two children because you and your partner are happy and fulfilled with that, then amend your progress accordingly. The goal to have children remains but the quantum changes – meaning that you will still achieve your objective. If the goal changes altogether (i.e. deciding not to have children), this will need serious consideration because that will mean no achievement against that goal and the objective will not be satisfied. Therefore, think hard about what you want – which is why time and honesty are crucial to the process to define your PDP and PrDP.

As you update your progress for each goal you will see the progress change and its resulting impact to your success story. This measuring and monitoring process will illustrate to you how close you are to achieving your goal(s), then objective(s) – and by inference – your PDP and PrDP.

The value of this tool is that it creates awareness within you over the value that you are creating or destroying for yourself with your day-to-day actions. Unfocussed actions and behaviours will not take you closer to your success story and will give you less time each day to get your vision of success. If you continue in this manner, only part of your success story will be realized (still better than none), which will invoke other emotions within you – not all positive.

Note that the tool caters for the duplication impact by correctly allocating the priority at the beginning of the exercise. In this way, you will have a more realistic view of your progress and perceived value gained.

A calculation spreadsheet such as MS Excel or similar will be best to use for measuring and monitoring because it will cut your administration time and direct your focus towards the prize – your success story.

Part 4: Becoming Your Best Self

Arguably the scariest part of the process is to start acting on your prioritized goals. For me, it was the anxiety around the high confidence but no guarantee that my plan would work that increased my anxiety. I faced a myriad of emotions through my processes when I reached this stage each time. I'm sure that many may feel this way too, while others are less anxious about what they have developed and more anxious to get going with your goals.

The reality is that there are no guarantees in life and for some reason we tend to want validation from others before trusting ourselves. As previously mentioned, when I looked around me, it was only my immediate family that stood firm to support. Most people we ready to trash my decisions, but none of them ever undertook such an exercise or been involved with such changes before. My thoughts were that if they did not undergo such before, they are probably in a less strengthened position than I was because I had the benefit of the life plan and all the effort that went into developing the plan. Also, having not done something similar before, they could not know better about my undertaking. Why then should I wait for their validation, surely it made more sense to take their advice and use it to help me succeed, where practicable, with my undertaking? Interesting perspective and very comforting for me. My stance was that I made a decision to be my best self and make big decisions. There could be no bigger decision than my future and I would rather aspire to be better and fall short than not aspire at all. If I fall short, I will still be many steps closer to my best self and would have feedback on improvements needed.

After taking some earlier advice, I backed myself and decided to take my first action towards my life plan. I recommend addressing any emotion and/or anxiety immediately so that these don't surface later and distract you. Addressing these does not mean that the anxiety and emotion will go away, it means that you will be able to deal with it while pushing forward. As you grow, the anxiety will diminish.

Dealing With the Emotions Around Your Life Plan

This is the stage where you look back at what you've done, marvel at the product, feel a sense of pride and then get scared again. If this is how you respond – don't worry because it is perfectly acceptable. Everything that you have done until now is planning and with your life experiences you would be abundantly aware that plans change. What we also know is that most plans do not change drastically and there are some plans that change very little.

Regardless of how you feel about your life plan, this is also the stage where you (like me) start to consider if the plan can actually work, if it is that simple and if you are destined for greatness – because, after all, not everybody is destined for greatness. I do not subscribe to that mindset. I believe destiny to be a real concept but I do not accept that we are all not destined for greatness. Recall that the intent of the life plan is to make you into the best version of yourself and not to make you "the best". If your best self is the best, then this will be an adventure of note.

If your best self does not take you to the point where you are the best, it's time to recognize that you have grown in stature and skill, you developed yourself further and have more capacity to grow. Life gave you feedback that it is not your time for reward because there is more to come for you. It will be time to buckle up and challenge yourself further. If you continue with this growth, you will have achieved greatness because you will have upskilled yourself to become the best version of yourself. Sadly, a large number of people give up after they implement some development practice but don't get the promotion, title or reward(s) that they anticipated. I noted that many gave up before reflecting on how much progress they actually made towards their prize. My thoughts were always that if they had done some reflection, perhaps their progress would have motivated them to persevere. I share Usain Bolt's sentiment that he took five years to run sub ten seconds but some people give up after a few months. Success takes time, discipline, skill and effort – there are many books that demonstrate this point many times over so I prefer to use their collective wisdom – because it makes sense to me. Your life plan demonstrates a path that targets growth, skill and development, which, with the requisite time and effort, will make you eligible to fight for your prize. I consider the time parameter as feedback that you have grown but your vision of success needs more work than you initially planned before you reap rewards.

There were also many situations where I observed individuals under pressure to comply with societal standards of success and/or greatness, instead of what they wanted. In most cases, the individual wanted other achievements and not the achievements that they were chasing. It was peculiar to see individuals fighting for what they did not want and were treating themselves as failures for not accomplishing what they did not want in the first place. This remains mind boggling for every time that I reflect on those observations.

I am reminded of another scenario where I witnessed friends and colleagues that marvel at others' achievements. My view is that we see many people who reach their goals and success stories daily, but we do not see the time, effort and other aspects of their success stories. The iceberg principle, **Figure 16**, has been used frequently to illustrate the relationship between effort and reward. Aside from its frequency of use, its message remains relevant and needs consideration.

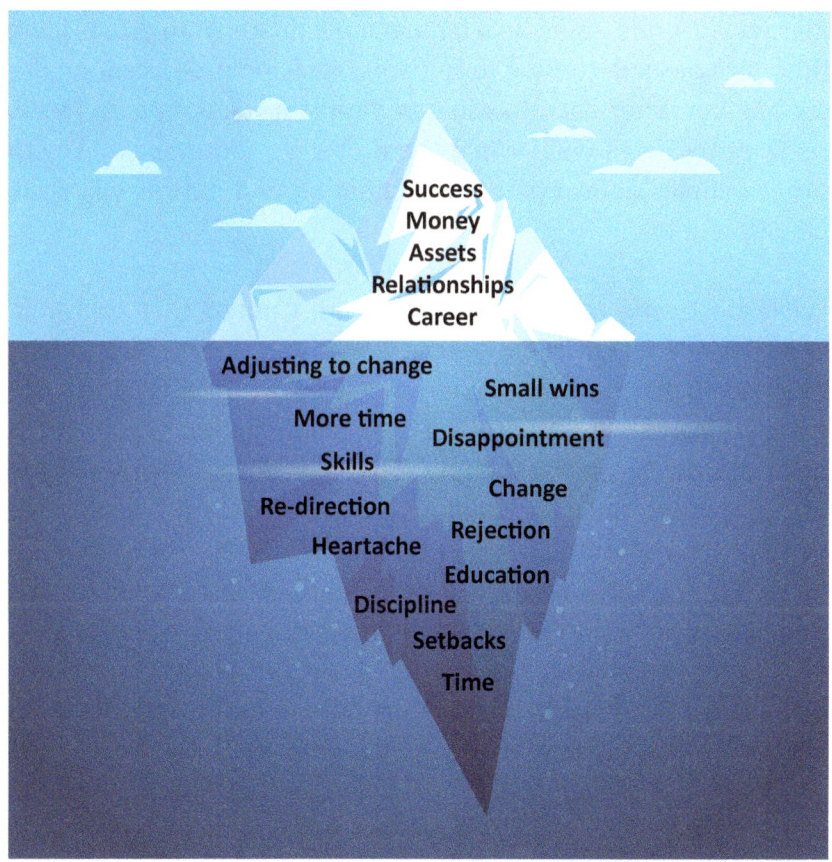

Figure 16 - Iceberg Principle as Foundation for Success

Figure 16 shows that the part of the iceberg exposed cannot exist without its base. Evidently, the base is much larger than the exposed bit and takes more effort to establish. If the base is weak, the iceberg will fracture and wither away. For me, the iceberg principle eloquently illustrates how much of the journey to success is overlooked. Rarely will somebody be an overnight success without proper effort to build capability and capacity. While we often miss this capacity and capability building phase, we will also be unaware of their progress in building their capacity and capability. My experience is that only the individual that is on the journey will understand how far that individual is from establishing their firm base. Returning to icebergs, each looks different on the surface but what each has in common is a rugged base. This is relevant to life as well. While there may be commonalities with other peoples' journeys, their destination and desires will likely be different.

While observing many similar journeys, I noted that each had different ideas for their success and that there was plenty of opportunity for those that are willing to fight for the right opportunity. While others may appear to be fighting for a similar prize, you don't know their story so avoid making a decision about your life based on their actions. I did the very same thing many times and was surprised to learn that our destinations were often very different. Fortunately, I did not abandon my journey (I backed myself and trusted the process) and reached my vision of success only to find the destination almost deserted. While I was happy because I achieved my objectives, my realization was that even though I saw many people on a similar journey as me, only a very small number shared the same destination as I did. Using the word "deserted" gives you some idea of the size of opportunity that existed at my destination relative to the number of people with the same vision of success.

Accept that there are other people with similar thoughts and plans, so somebody is going to reap a reward – why should it not be you? Also accept that there are fewer people than you think who are fighting for the same reward/prize that you are targeting. With an effective plan, the right focus and discipline, you could be the next person to reap the reward. My message will always be to back yourself, trust the process, persevere and move forward.

Here's another point of view worth considering: how do you know if you are destined for greatness if you don't start living your best life? I am also going to add that we generally listen to other people's opinions form their observations, their research and most importantly – their biases. We do not always know the intentions of the people that we encounter. While I believe in the human spirit, my experience showed that every person is focused on what is best for them. Only a precious few will put the needs of others ahead or even on par with theirs. My message here is that we should take feedback from people as advice, but make up our own minds to realize our vision of success.

I adopt the mindset that value is easy to identify if you have clarity for what you are searching. Armed with your vision, skills and knowledge (sometimes needing permission when intellectual property matters surface) all that is missing is discipline and action – factors that are entirely under our control. My focus therefore has always been on being a better person today than I was yesterday and act to be a better person tomorrow than I am today. This, in my opinion, is being great – so why is greatness unattainable by more people than we currently encounter? This is a challenge that I undertook and encourage you to take this leap of faith as well. After all, you did the hard work and laid the foundation meaning that you are ready to build.

While I hope this would motivate you, I will share that I too was nervous and scared with what I developed as my life plan. The thought hit home for me that I had some big decisions to make, prime among them was if I was prepared to take action on my life plan instead of relegating the plan to yet another theoretical and/or academic exercise. I chose to push forward with my plan because I was (and still remain) sure that I wanted to be a better version of myself and continue to improve on being a better version each day forward. That meant sacrifice, (calculated) risks and action. This journey remains scary and will challenge your paradigm, but if you choose to push forward, this will likely be among your top five best decisions – it certainly was for me.

Time to Get Going – the Most Important First Step
Considerations When Taking Your First Step

Taking the first step to action the life plan will be an important obstacle to clear and has everything to do with re-programming your mindset. I took my first step once I framed my purpose very clearly. I'm reminded of Robin Sharma's "The Monk Who Sold His Ferrari" when I think about framing one's purpose. If you focus on the material world and titles without improving your personal self, you will find yourself in poor health, void of meaningful relationships and with a certain emptiness that is akin to loneliness or depression. Be honest with yourself and whether you want to make the necessary changes towards a more fulfilling life that you can look back upon and be proud of for yourself. Use this principle to focus your mind towards implementing your newly defined life plan – it's worth the effort, more importantly, YOU'RE worth the effort. Robin Sharma offers a great perspective on identifying whether you are living your best life, how to understand your purpose, understand what true value is for you and understand what success means to you. To achieve this, you must understand where you are in life and then take the necessary action to change for the better.

In his other book "Lead without a title", Robin Sharma shares the value of taking charge of important actions that are in the best interest of companies, jobs, relationships and roles. Among the many messages that Robin Sharma offers, the idea of not waiting for permission to do the right thing right the first time and doing your best regardless of who is watching without consideration of reward, resonates with me. The relevance to this book and process is that you do not need anybody's permission to become your best self. You certainly do not need to wait for somebody to tell you that you should or when you should. Once you decide to become your best self, do not wait – act and grow.

Using Robin Sharma's message and your life plan, you will have realised another obstacle – how do you change your beliefs and thoughts that may be holding you back or slowing you down. Anthony Robbins does an excellent job of defining how to challenge your paradigms and reset your mindset in his book "Awaken the Giant Within". The summarized version is that it works best to record your thoughts and views about yourself and your beliefs. Then take each belief and challenge it critically until you understand its origins and the validity of the factors feeding that belief. When you address the dysfunctionality of the factors feeding your belief and the belief itself, you will have freed yourself to amend that belief. Anthony Robbins takes you on a journey to establish new and functional beliefs that will contribute to being your best self. I strongly recommend sourcing the book to go through the exercise so that you are best positioned to get you to your vision of success. Again, this is not about being self-absorbed or self-centred, it is all about being clear to yourself about the person that you are or want to become and how to make that person into a functional positive member in all your relationships.

Do not under-estimate the value of challenging your paradigms and going through Anthony Robbins' exercises. The results may surprise you but will take you to a point where you will have to make some hard decisions to replace certain beliefs and practices with more functional and strong-rooted beliefs and practices. This is a very necessary step because only once you root out the non-performing components of your life – either replace, eradicate or improve – will you start to see real results. Ken Blanchard in his book "Winning" offers real life examples to demonstrate the value of addressing under-performing elements once you have a clear vision of where you are heading. Even though this is applied to the corporate world, recognize that you are the CEO of your life and wholly accountable for the results.

Exercise caution to make sure that you are challenging your beliefs towards becoming a better version of yourself and NOT using it as a means to break important bonds (e.g. with immediate family) and shirk your responsibilities. This is a sensitive topic outside this book, but these relationships will be evident to you.

Taking the First Step

The process thus far will help you to make the decision to embark on the journey towards your best self, aided by the tools and models shared within the book. While making the decision to proceed is the first step, the elephant in the room is always around the first action that should be taken to kick-start your journey. During my journey, I often leapt into the detail only to surface sometime later to assess what I actually achieved. There were times when I was proud of what I had achieved and other times when I was unsure if I added value or not. Before sounding the alarm bells, there is a simple action that can be implemented to avoid this time wastage.

This action is already well known to many people and entails identifying key activities to complete leading to an achievement then scheduling these with relationships, but seldom considered because it appears complex. To cut the technical jargon, yes, it is about putting a schedule or project plan of sorts to guide your actions while maintaining focus on the big picture.

My 2004 revelation was an opportune moment in my journey. Having been in industry for a few years by that time and having been exposed to the world of project management, I used some of that knowledge for my journey. The concept of planning, scheduling and activities appealed to me but applied differently. There was no need to have a detailed plan as is adopted for industry projects. A more functional approach would be to work with a higher-level idea of how much time you want to give yourself for your journey, when you would like to reach your goal and some important events along your journey. For my journey, I defined my important milestones to be (with example durations indicated alongside each milestone):

- Prepare schedule to create my life plan: 7 days.
- Complete brainstorming: 91 days.
- Finalize objectives: 14 days.
- Define goals: 14 days.
- Prioritize tasks and actions: 7 days.
- Start actioning my life plan: 0 days.

Note: the durations based on spending thirty to sixty minutes per day to get to the 3-Page Plan. My durations were different – as you would have gathered from my accounts – but were achieved by spending at least forty-five minutes per day on my journey to develop my 3-Page Plan. I used indicative durations above to simplify the calculation for the book, but these were the milestones that I used for my process. My rationale was that the schedule was *another tool to use for my life plan so my focus would be best directed towards the life plan and not distracted by any tool for any period of time. I kept my schedule to take my first step simple (six activities) to illustrate the importance of the process and focusing on (Stephen Covey's) "end". Focusing on any particular tool for too long did not work for me because I lost interest after a while and took a long time to return to the plan. After initially complicating my process and being too detailed with the tools, I felt that I was fooling myself, which increased my frustrations. I encourage you to keep things as simple as possible, which was an important lesson for me. After simplifying my timeline, I developed the schedule illustrated in **Figure 17** and **Figure 18**. There is no need to use formal project scheduling software; a simple Gantt chart or even illustration on a spreadsheet will suffice. Remember, this "first steps" schedule plots the path and duration that identifies your first step and following steps to get to your life plan. It does not plot the path and duration to achieve your vision of success, because this plan and timeline will emerge upon completing the "first steps" schedule.*

Figure 17 illustrates the duration to develop your life plan, while **Figure 18** shows that duration converted to a date. From **Figure 17**, the overall duration to develop a life plan works out to 20 calendar weeks (based on the durations that I used above). This will be different for each person and is based on your objectives, your preference for effort that you want to spend per milestone, your preferred time for reflection and the time you consume while soliciting feedback from your inner and trusted circles. I used these timelines because I observed that shorter timelines did not deliver useful results because the focus was placed on finishing rather than value. If you are able to finish faster, good on you and you will start your journey sooner. While you have time to get this done properly, rushing the process will be futile because this is not a race – it is a marathon. Taking too much time will also be futile because you will create too many distractions and lose the benefit of the life plan process. Recall that the durations were based on spending thirty to sixty minutes per day. If you are able to spend more time, then the duration will be shorter but the time related to the effort will be similar. If you spend shorter than thirty minutes per day, there is strong likelihood that you experience more momentum interruptions that will render the process ineffective. The message here is that continuity, effort and discipline must be balanced when developing your 3-Page Plan.

I understand that this may sound cryptic, but there can be no prescribed timeline to develop a meaning life plan to achieve your vision of success. My experience showed that five months was the minimum time to develop a meaningful life plan and ten months was the maximum time. Again, based on spending thirty to sixty minutes per day to develop your 3-Page Plan. There were some whom developed their plan faster (not many) but those that consumed longer than ten months stopped their process mostly because it was too detailed and each person lost the appetite to proceed with the detail that they created. I also observed that those who took longer than ten months either over-thought their process, psyched themselves out of proceeding or did not see sufficient value created over that time – then opting to abandon the process. Yet another reason to keep things simple.

To complete the discussion, **Figure 18** illustrates that if you start the life plan in the first week of January and adhere to the durations indicated, you will have a completed 3-Page Plan that is ready to action on the 19 May – based on the time spent per day proviso. This is the timeline to develop your 3-Page Plan and give you an idea for when you can start working on your prioritized tasks and actions associated with your goals. It is not when you will achieve your success story, because that will be determined by your objectives and goals.

Completing the 3-Page Plan via this schedule offers a simple master-plan to guide your actions along your journey. The schedule will be a constant visual reminder of your commitment and, hopefully, inspire you to accelerate your journey. I found this useful during my journey because of the schedule's simplicity and significantly less detail than most project schedules that I used to manage.

Activity #	Activity Descirption	Duration (Calendar Days)
1	Prepare schedule to create my life plan	7
2	Complete brainstorming	91
3	Finalize objectives	14
4	Define goals	14
5	Prioritize tasks and actions	7
6	Start actioning my life	0

Figure 17 - Indicative Schedule Duration to Develop My Life Plan

Activity #	Activity Descirption	Duration (Calendar Days)
1	Prepare schedule to create my life plan	7
2	Complete brainstorming	91
3	Finalize objectives	14
4	Define goals	14
5	Prioritize tasks and actions	7
6	Start actioning my life	0

January				Febuary				March					April				May		
7	14	21	28	4	11	18	25	3	10	17	24	31	7	14	21	28	5	12	19

Figure 18 - Indicative Schedule Dates to Develop My Life Plan

Moving to the Second Step and Beyond

When I reached this stage of development, I was particularly proud of my achievement. But I started to feel an uneasiness over the process and next steps. Having returned to my plan, it was a stark reality from the progress measurement aspect, that I made little to no progress on my plan.

After spending a few days mulling why I hadn't made the progress that I had intended, even though I had learned all the tools, my obstacle became clear. I understood the tools, their value and how to use the tools – but I did not address my habits until that point. I started to understand the subtle but glaring difference between beliefs and habits. Beliefs feed your habits but both need work if you want real change. I had adjusted my beliefs, but did not address my habits, and saw that within a short period of time, I started to return to my old ways. I took one step forward but stayed exactly where I was!

It was irritating to realise that I had delivered wasted effort to myself because most of my effort for change through the life plan was negated for the simple reason that old habits truly die hard. This was, for me, the second step where I spent many days trying to adjust habits, discover new habits and alter behaviour. I even stumbled across ways and means to reinforce certain behaviours and minimise others. All worked well and after some time I was able to start driving my life plan with more intent, which led to positive results. While I'm a strong advocate for purposeful action, I'm also an advocate for smart action. Instead of sharing what I've done to address my "old habits", I prefer to share a more effective technique than what I used at that time. The concept of "Atomic Habits" by James Clear is remarkably simple but effective to address undesired habits. The principle is that small changes every day will compound to give you higher value returns. The trick lies in identifying the undesired habits and what could be desired habits. James Clear will take you on a journey to address these for yourself. "Atomic Habits" will show you how to replace habits, but you will need to do some serious introspection to define your undesired habits and what could be desired habits for you. The book offers good pointers for this so you won't be left stranded with more "what" questions.

At this point, let's understand where we are with your picture for success through a short recap,

- You have your 3-Page Plan.
- You understand the value of striving for a more meaningful life.
- You understand that the decision to be a better version of yourself rests solely with you and you do not need anybody else's permission to be the best version of yourself.
- You adjusted your belief system to grow towards the best version of yourself.
- You know how to amend your habits as you adjusted your belief system.

If by now you are convinced that you are equipped for the subsequent steps, you are on a spring board and about to launch – which is exhilarating. If you have not taken any of the steps until now, you are probably holding yourself back in some shape or manner. This is different from changing your paradigms, as Anthony Robbins demonstrates, and has more to do with certain behaviours that need to be advanced while others need to be changed. The good news is that you have means to address these behaviours and habits. As always, holding yourself to account for your own life will be important. To address the behavioural/habitual aspects of the process, I found that adopting a leadership journal was a vital action. Many historical leaders, e.g. Sir Winston Churchill and I am sure many current leaders, adopted the leadership journal with encouraging results. The leadership journal is geared for you to identify behaviours and actions that you consider to be counter-productive to what you are trying to achieve. The approach works because it aims to establish a written and visual account of your progress in addressing these changes. It is a useful tool that links well with this book and James Clear's concept of Atomic Habits. This process starts with identifying for yourself aspects of your everyday behaviour that you feel are counter-productive and then defining a positive behaviour that you would like to adopt in place of that behaviour (atomic habits).

To share how I incorporated the leadership journal with Atomic Habits, I identified a list of behaviours that were on the top of my mind and through feedback that I received from my inner circle as a starting point. Once done, I chose one to three of the high priority behaviours that I believed needed addressing. The key is to be clear and concise on the behaviour to be adjusted, e.g. "I want to stop interrupting people before they finish what they have to say; within 4 weeks". After recording the behaviour(s) to be addressed, at the end of each day I reflected on my day and recorded the instances when I interrupted people. I found that recording the day and date and then numbering the incidents for that day was most effective for me. To help your journey, you may opt to keep a book with you to record the instances during the day and transcribe the incidents during your evening reflection. Done right, the reflection and recording should not take longer than ten minutes. The technique is based on reflection and feedback – so you should consider asking for input from your trusted inner circle members. Make sure that they are aware of your journey and are willing to share their observations – if they were in your presence through the day. The inner circle members will help to point out the times that you repeat the counter-productive behaviour as further input. The technique is effective for two reasons, namely, it creates awareness with discipline within you about you, and it is a visual reminder of your actions. Having made the decision to grow into a better version of yourself, you will note the high number of times that you repeat the counter-productive action daily. As you continue with the exercise over the days ahead, you will note the frequency with which you repeat this behaviour. Within a short period of time your sub-conscious will kick in to drive you to improve your behaviour until you reduce the frequency of interrupting people to, at most, once or twice. If this is the tolerance that you set for yourself, you've achieved your goal. If not, continue until you achieve your tolerance – but be sure not to sabotage yourself with unreasonable tolerances because this will destroy value.

As you move to the next behaviour to address, keep the addressed behaviour as a reminder so you prevent regressing into the that behaviour at a later stage. I would recommend reading Sri Satya Sai Sadhana Trust Publications' "The Mahavakya's of Leadership" or a similar book, to get a good account of the exercise. Within the book are other effective leadership tools to help grow yourself. Be aware that this is a book from a religious organization, but the principles are sound. If you prefer to refrain from sourcing religious books, search for the "leadership journal" and "Winston Churchill" to identify where you can source other texts that demonstrate this technique.

Once you developed the motivation to take action, understand that motivation only gets you to the game, discipline and smart work keeps you in the game. That statement is as cryptic as I first heard or read from many leadership experts. Simply put, if you want sustainable results, you have to keep working on your identified actions and goals daily to improve yourself to get closer to your success story.

The value to you will be experienced through your 3-Page Plan because it brings the process to better yourself together with the tools to implement that plan. The 3-Page Plan is simple and can be carried with you or displayed as a constant reminder. The more you see it, the more likely you are to execute the plan – keep this in mind as part of taking action.

Reminder: if your goals don't scare you, you're not thinking big enough!

Part 5: Take Stock and Adjust

This chapter is not about reviewing or adjusting your 3-Page Plan prior to implementing. That will be an exercise in futility because of the tremendous thought that you put into developing your plan. This chapter is about dealing with the challenges that life will throw at your plan because the 3-Page Plan is not immune to challenges. Having developed your 3-Page Plan and taken some action, you will have built the skills and capacity to address these challenges and continue moving forward.

The measuring and monitoring tool was helpful for most challenges, but some challenges escalated as life changed around me. My best response was to avoid the knee-jerk reaction to abandon my plan but rather adjust some elements of my plan based on analysing the outcomes and advice from my inner circle and trusted circle.

I sometimes found myself trying to make adjustments too quickly because I was looking for instant gratification from some actions. In one instance I considered drastic changes to my 3-Page Plan. Coincidentally, I had an engagement with one of my mentors where I shared, among other things, the event in mind and my intended changes. After going into "coach mode" to simplify the matter with me, I realized that I completely missed my blind-spots and magnified small issues. I was so focused on one particular aspect, that I glossed over the value that I had already received. During that time, I also forgot that I structured some goals as building blocks to other goals and some objectives. The big-ticket item that I was targeting was one of those goals and needed more time to be achieved. I paid little attention to the partial benefits as I progressed with that goal.

Following the engagement with my mentor, I made no changes to my 3-Page Plan but relooked at some actions and the timeline for that goal. After adjusting the route to that goal, I achieved the goal and objective, but will share that I felt that I could have received more benefit had I followed original plan.

The event described indicated that my 3-Page Plan was far from perfect but it was an excellent platform to build real capacity and skills. After some achievements, I was able to amend my plan slightly but kept the objectives and goals unchanged. I added tasks, amended details of tasks, revised some sequences for tasks and adjusted some timelines. These actions targeted the lowest level of the 3-Page Plan and did not affect my "destination".

Aside from minor adjustments to your plan, as you progress, you will reach the point where you will ask the obvious question: "what next?" This question will surface if your plan is delivering the intended benefits to you to the point that you achieved all or most of your objectives; or if the plan is not working and you have not experienced sufficient benefits. If your life plan worked for you, you may want to consider challenging yourself further. If you choose to stop developing further once you achieve your life plan, that is entirely up to you, be wary that you risk growing restless after experiencing the benefits gained. If you choose to continue developing yourself further, the next chapter will offer some insight to you. I will always advocate for continuous development because I believe that we should always aim to be a better version of ourselves tomorrow than we are today.

In the case where your 3-Page Plan has not delivered your expected value, there exists some aspect(s) that needs attention.

Your time will be best spent to return to your plan then reflect on what you are doing and the changes that have occurred – positive and negative. While doing this, reflect on what you are actually doing versus what you targeted to do as part of your goals and actions. Be honest with yourself and critically analyse your findings – do not defend because you will only be lying to yourself.

I received comments from people who believed that the 3-Page Plan did not work for them. Some were willing to engage but most preferred to keep to themselves. When I engaged the few that wanted to discuss their results, we realized that there were some elements that added little value. In most cases those elements were "popular choices" as opposed to a choice that resonated with the individual. Mostly, there was insufficient thought put into the individual's vision for a successful life. Limiting themselves at that early stage, led to limitations with their goals and objectives, culminating with benefits that were inadequately defined and, in some cases, unwanted.

These were difficult but necessary conversations that produced different responses. Disappointingly, those that abandoned their 3-Page Plan did not recognise the benefits they received while implementing their plan. I would like to believe that had those individuals recognized the benefits received, they may have been inspired to revisit their plan, describe their vision of success clearer then define their objectives and goals in a more functional manner.

I will accept that this process is not perfect. What I have seen is that being clear and honest with myself was a critical pre-requisite for the process. Rewards were proportional to my effort such that when I spent quality time developing plans with sufficient detail, I experienced more value from my actions. The level of detail when describing plans is a subjective matter. What worked for me was to get to the level of detail where I was able to predict the outcome of any plan – not the final result. For example, qualifying with an MBA degree capacitated me to get more involved with corporate finance and corporate strategy as my outcome. Adding more detail to identify the exact portfolio where I would use my MBA skills to influence the financing strategy was what I considered as too detailed (the result).

The lesson in this chapter is that plans work when adequate thought and action are embedded with taking accountability for those plans, its intended value and actions. Nobody knows everything but if you have a solid base with good support, you are likely to cover most matters that need to be addressed. The other stumbling block is over-thinking your plan because this creates unnecessary complexity. I almost fell into this trap and discovered that I created plans to address matters that will never surface. Some matters had a slim chance of occurring but somebody managed to make a compelling argument that convinced me otherwise. Against my better judgement I developed plans to address these matters, which was a waste of time and a source of frustration. When I reflect on those instances, had I reverted to my definition of who I was (**Table 1 - Example of results for a self-reflection exercise**) and my paradigm for what I wanted (**Figure 4 - The compromise for when defining what I wanted**), I would have recognised that those were background noise matters and I would have likely discarded them.

Before making changes, ensure that you have proper data to analyse, compare to your expectations and then make changes. Actions without data amounts to speculation, which can be disastrous. When things do not work to plan, accept that it may be time to be clear on why things did not work – using the data and that you have – and make adjustments (again, using your data). Journeys seldom work exactly to plan but the destination remains unchanged.

Finally, if you are going to be afraid to "fail" you will also not achieve your vision of success. If that is satisfactory for you, then that is entirely your choice. If you desire growth and aspire to being your best self, you will need to take calculated risks while demonstrating accountability for yourself to yourself.

Part 6: The Extended/Advanced Life Plan

Should your plan have delivered the expected value or if your plan did not deliver the expected value but you want to persevere, this chapter is for you. The subtle difference is that some people may opt to stop once completing their original 3-Page Plan – regardless of the results. If you would like to take steps to elevate yourself further, this chapter offers a brief explanation of what I found to be useful.

In the case of your plan having worked for you and you wanting to better yourself further, repeat Step 1 and Step 2 to define what is next for you. I recommend using your current 3-Page Plan to ensure that you build on what you have achieved instead of going backwards. By "build what you have achieved", I refer to your vision of success – not the exercise to build your 3-Page Plan. The idea is to be a better version of yourself so pick-up from where you are and build better. This will create renewed vigour to inspire you to continue elevating yourself. Be sure to define the "why" for what you want very clearly to avoid the risk of repeating previous objectives. Once done, follow the process outlined in section 5. The point of the extended or advance life plan is to establish a new set of objectives and goals that are bigger and more challenging. This time, the process will be faster and easier having done it before.

In the case that your original life plan did not work out well for you, start by taking stock if your actions align with your goals, if your goals align with the objectives and if changes are needed.

You will need to be honest with yourself and critically analyse your findings. I experienced this through my journey and discovered that I developed my first 3-Page Plan in isolation and with limited knowledge. It was quite irritating because of the time and effort that I put into the plan without the reward(s) – to the point that I largely ignored the plan for years. Then in 2004 after interacting with my mentors, I started to understand how little I actually knew about life and the value of experience. I returned to the objectives setting but this time solicited input from seven senior people with various qualifications and roles. The common traits among them were that they were well experienced (ten years to forty years) and most had multi-industry experience with multiple different companies. Their perspectives were insightful and shed a level of thinking that I did not contemplate. After completing my updated 3-Page Plan, I discussed the plan with three trusted mentors, who gave me great advice on tweaks. Having made those tweaks – I was more confident of the new 3-Page Plan that showed better alignment and insight.

To illustrate the plan's value for decision making, I was extremely comfortable at the company that I worked for at the time. Even received accolades and recognition from senior executives consistently. However, when I completed my 2004 3-Page Plan, it was clear that in my role at that time, I would not be able to achieve my vision of success and I had to search for alternative employment to satisfy my inner most desires. This was risky, but I used the new plan as a decision-making tool – after all, it had the combined knowledge of greater than 120 years from my seven mentors – which was enough mitigation for me. The alternative at that time was to stay where I was and wonder what could have been. Fast forward 21 years, I am living my success story, completing the last goal to my final objective – being this book – and moving onto my advanced life plan with no regrets.

Regardless of the scenario, be sure to keep your original 3-Page Plan for periodic reference but implement your advanced or extended 3-Page Plan and display the plan in the most visual manner possible. You will have matured since the first 3-Page Plan, so the original plan will be a reminder to you to persevere and of the value that awaits you at the end of the journey.

Closing Remarks

As you reach the end of this book, know that it is not merely a theoretical exercise that I share with you. In the early days of the plan, I did not have the benefit of many of the tools and books referenced to guide my thinking. As I learnt more techniques and tools, I implemented them with my plan and learnt many lessons along the way. In doing so, it was clear that the constant for the plan was the process and approach. My take away was that any tool, model, framework or technique could be used to address the exercises described within the book. The real value is the result from whatever model, tool, technique and/or framework that you use because the process and approach use the results to deliver your 3-Page Plan.

Through my personal and professional life, I had the privilege of sharing the concept for My Life Plan, the 3-Page Plan process and the approach with my immediate family, friends, colleagues and those that I coached/mentored. Each time I was pleasantly surprised by the value that this approach generated and the introspection that it inspired within those that chose to take up the challenge. Most started the exercise but few took the exercise to completion. I can happily say that those that took the exercise to completion had a new perspective on their life with renewed vigour. Those that opted to stop the exercise received some value in that they looked at life differently and (what I believe to be) in a more positive and focused manner.

It is true that the hardest conversation that we will ever have will be the conversation that we have with ourselves. It is not easy to accept our limitations – even though we are all aware that we have limitations – and even harder to take action to address these limitations. Within this book I offer to you my journey to address my limitations and happily confirm to you that once I climbed that mountain, I found yet another mountain. This time, the new mountain was higher, steeper and with more obstacles – but the summit looks magnificent. At the time of print, I started climbing the new mountain and used the extended/advanced life plan approach to chart my climb. It appears that the extended/advanced life plan is a magnet for all obstacles, but the gratification after clearing each obstacle makes the journey all the more exciting.

Brace yourself for the various stages of development. The magnitude of your vision of success will make this a long journey. Do not be swayed by the time needed relative to where you are, rather take the first step and then start to reflect on your achievements (however small or big) because these will motivate you to go further. It is true that you will encounter more rejections than acceptance as you grow and extend yourself. This is normal because people are in general cautious when they encounter anything new or different. Keep persevering because each rejection is feedback that will direct you to where your value belongs and where you will best apply yourself.

I sincerely hope that you are inspired by what I shared within this book and choose to take up the challenge. If you do, all the best to you for your journey to your vision of success (and hopefully success stories). If you choose not to take up the challenge, many thanks for your patience and all the best to you as well.

References

"Who moved my cheese?"
"Awaken the giant within"
"The monk who sold his Ferrari"
"Lead without a title"
"Surrounded by idiots"
"The 5 love languages"
"The 7 habits for highly effective people"
"Personal branding"
"Mahavakya's of leadership"
"Winning"

www.ingramcontent.com/pod-product-compliance
Lightning Source LLC
Chambersburg PA
CBHW051130160426
43195CB00014B/2416